Domestic buildings at Chepstow, Gwent

CASTLES OF GWENT, GLAMORGAN & GOWER

Mike Salter

FOLLY PUBLICATIONS

ACKNOWLEDGEMENTS

The photographs in this book were taken by the author, and old postcards are reproduced from those in his collection. The author also drew the map and the plans, which are mostly reproduced on scales of 1:400, 1:800, 1:2000, and are modified or improved versions of surveys he has made over the years, including a number used for an A-level thesis whilst a pupil at Wolverhampton Grammar School (1965-72). Thanks are due to Helen Thomas for driving on several recent trips to take extra photos for this new edition, and also to Ian Rennie, who drove on one of the trips.

This book is dedicated to the memory of G.T.Clark and Sidney Toy, whose books first inspired the author to measure and draw plans and sections of medieval castles.

AUTHOR'S NOTES

The title used for the original 1991 edition of this book has been retained despite the fact that the name Monmouthshire has been reinstated for most of the area then known as Gwent. For convenience of visitors Gower is divided off from Glamorgan with its own gazetteer, this reflecting the medieval lordship pattern in South Wales.

This series of books (see full list inside back cover) are intended as portable field guides giving as much information and illustrative material as possible in volumes of modest size, weight and price. The aim in the castle books has been to mention, where the information is known to the author, owners or custodians who were the first or last of a line to hold an estate, an important office, or a title. Those in occupation at the time of dramatic events such as sieges or royal visits and those who made alterations or additions are also often named. Due to the constraints of space owners and occupants of medieval castles whose lives had little effect on the condition of the buildings are not often mentioned, nor are most 19th and 20th century events (unless particularly dramatic), nor ghost stories or legends.

The books are intended to be used in conjunction with the Ordnance Survey 1:50,000 maps. Grid references are given in the gazetteers, together with a coding system explaining what sort of public access (if any) is available, which is explained on page 112. Maps will be required to find most of the lesser-known sites.

Each level of a building is called a storey in this book, the basement being the first or lowest storey with its floor near courtyard level unless mentioned as otherwise. The buildings were measured in metres and metric scales and dimensions are used throughout the book. Three metres is almost ten feet for those who need to convert to imperial scales. In most cases dimensions are external at or near ground level, but above a plinth or battered base if there is one. On plans original work is black, post 1800 work is stippled, and medieval alterations and additions are shown hatched.

ABOUT THE AUTHOR

Mike Salter is 49 and has been a professional writer and publisher since he went on the Government Enterprise Allowance Scheme for unemployed people in 1988. He is particularly interested in the planning and layout of medieval buildings. Wolverhampton born and bred, Mike now lives in an old cottage beside the Malvern Hills. He other interests include walking, maps, railways, board games, morris dancing, and playing percussion instruments with an occasional ceilidh band.

Copyright Mike Salter 1991 & 2002. Original first edition first published June 1991. This totally revised new edition with extra illustrations published December 2002. Folly Publications, Folly Cottage, 151 West Malvern Rd, Malvern, Worcs WR14 4AY. Printed by Aspect Design, 89 Newtown Rd, Malvern, Worcs WR14 2PD.

St Donat's Castle, Glamorgan

CONTENTS

Lists of extra sites appear at the end of each gazetteer.
Maps of the sites described appear inside the front cover.

INTRODUCTION

The type of defensible lordly residence known to the Normans as a castle was unknown in Wales before they invaded it. In 1067 William the Conqueror created an earldom of Hereford for his cousin William Fitz-Osbern with special privilages to rule that county with his own army and judiciary so as to create a strong buffer zone between England and Wales. Earl William was given leave to take whatever land he could from the Welsh and he built a castle at Chepstow, but was killed in Normandy in February 1071. King William advanced to St Davids in 1081 and is thought to have had the motte at Cardiff begun, but otherwise it was only after Rhys ap Tewdwr, ruler of Deheubarth, was killed near Brecon in 1093, that the Normans began to take over significant amounts of Welsh territory. Robert Fitz-Hamon, Lord of Gloucester, took over the castle at Cardiff as his chief seat and captured the fertile southern part of Morgannwg from Iestyn ap Gwrgant. Earl Robert granted most of these lands to knights who held their estates in return for military service to him. In time this feudal system of land-tenure was extended through Gwent and Gower also, the knights and their households forming a thin veneer of French-speaking Normans ruling from their castles a hostile and mostly Welsh-speaking populace. Those Welsh chiefs still surviving were banished to the upland regions. Gradually they too began to build castles and some of them adopted Norman names and customs, such as inheritance by primogeniture. Those that didn't throw in their lot with the Normans and adopt their ways were mostly ousted by the end of the 13th century.

The early castles were generally quickly and cheaply constructed of earth and wood by gangs of slave labourers with a minimum of skilled craftsmen. A common form comprised an earth mound or motte surmounted by a timber tower within a small palisaded court, and a bailey or larger court lower down with its own rampart, palisade and ditch surrounding a hall, chapel, workshops, stables, granary, and other farm buildings, all of wood or unmortared stone. The tower on the mound formed a private dwelling for the lord and a final refuge if the weaker bailey perimeter defences should be penetrated by a hostile force. The basic design varied according to the terrain, and the amount of labour and time available. A small enclosure with high banks (known to modern castle experts as a ringwork) was sometimes provided instead of a motte, and baileys were omitted or duplicated and laid out in whatever size and shape local circumstances dictated. Natural spurs and hillocks were used where possible, being shaped into steep-sided and level-topped mottes. Over 70 earthworks of these types survive in Gwent, Glamorgan and Gower, and a number of others have now been destroyed.

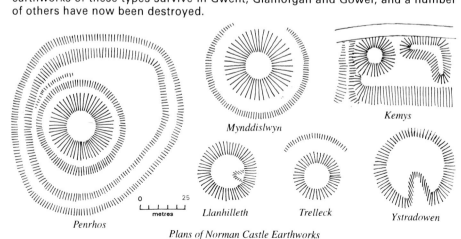

Mynddislwyn

Kemys

0   25
metres

Llanhilleth

Trelleck

Ystradowen

Penrhos

Plans of Norman Castle Earthworks

The shell keep at Cardiff Castle, Glamorgan   *Middle bailey gateway, Chepstow*

Although earth and wood were the normal materials for 11th century castles William Fitz-Osbern's castle on a rocky ridge at Chepstow had a stone hall block and two walled baileys, the earliest castle of its type in Britain, and one of only about twenty fortified in stone before the year 1100, another being Cardiff, where part of a Roman fort was adapted to form a bailey. The Chepstow hall block contained a poorly illuminated hall and chamber over an even darker basement. There are typically Norman pilaster buttresses at the corners and along the sides, and the entrance doorway was placed quite high up. The baileys were modest walled courts containing wooden buildings but without any of the towers or gatehouses now adorning them.

Chepstow remained the only castle in South Wales with a stone hall or keep for a generation. The similar structure at Monmouth and a smaller example at Ogmore may be of c1125. Several castles in Gower and Morgannwg were captured by the Welsh in 1116, and in 1158, 1172 and 1182 they were goaded into revolts causing damage to various castles. Henry II's Pipe Rolls record the garrison arrangements and repairs and improvements to several castles in Wales then in royal custody. Gradually combustible wooden palisades were replaced by stone walls and keeps. The stone encircling wall (known to modern writers as a shell keep), on the motte summit at Cardiff may be of c1135-40 and another was later built on the mound at Caerleon. By the 1190s there were square tower keeps with curtain walls on the mottes at Swansea and Llantilio (later known as White Castle), and Newcastle Bridgend had a curtain wall with two flanking towers surrounding a now-vanished keep. There were also substantial keeps at Dinas Powys, Kenfig, Sully, more modest examples at Fonmon, Penllyn and Oystermouth, and small examples at Penhow, Usk and St Donat's, which also had a walled court. Llanhilleth seems to have had a rare cross-shaped tower. Some of these keeps contained just one room for the lord over a basement but others had a more tower-like form with a separate living room and bedroom one above the other with a basement below. In each case the windows were small round-headed openings and the doorway was high above ground level with an approach by wooden steps. Grosmont has a block of c1200-5 which contained a fine hall and chamber over basement rooms and there was also a defensible hall block of about the same period at the Welsh castle of Baglan.

Ogmore Castle, Glamorgan

Circular towers, which have no blind or undermineable corners, appeared in Gwent in the 1190s when William Marshal, Earl of Pembroke added three of them to flank one of the baileys there. He or one of his sons later added an outer bailey with a twin-towered gatehouse. From c1212 William built walls with a series of circular towers at Usk, and another of the same decade survives at Caerleon. In the 1220s Hubert de Burgh, a leading magnate during King's John's reign and during the minority of Henry III, built walled courts at Grosmont and Skenfrith which made systematic use of round corner towers. Skenfrith also has a detached circular tower keep with a semi-circular turret on one side. A similar keep lies on a motte at one corner of the castle at Caldicot, begun by the de Bohun earl of Hereford also in the 1220s. Caldicot has one other round tower and two which are U-shaped, one a gatehouse and the other a solar block. Another circular keep added at Monmouth in the 1230s has vanished. Of the same period are cruder examples at Penrice, built by a Gower knight, and Castell Meredydd, built by a Welsh chieftain, and there are traces of others thought to be the work of Richard de Clare at Llantrisant and Talyfan. Neath has remains of a small court with two D-shaped towers. Not all curtain walls of this period had flanking towers. Those at Ogmore and Dinas Powis are probably of c1200-10, and those at Penhow, St Fagans, Penmark are probably of c1220-50.

Morgraig and Coch are thought to have formed part of Gilbert de Clare's schemes for securing his northern boundary. Coch has a small D-shaped court with a hall block and circular keep, with two other towers of similar size and a square gatehouse added later. Morgraig has a rectangular keep and four U-shaped towers set at the corners of a polygonal court. In 1266 Gilbert de Clare took the southern part of Senghenydd from its Welsh ruler and immediately began a new castle that set a new standard for military architecture in Britain. It has a quadrangular court of medium size with lofty round corner towers and a pair of twin-towered gatehouses set opposite each other. This court fills most of a platform with a high retaining wall rising from a lake created by building a long fortified dam across the width of a shallow valley. Built in two stages, the dam has twin-towered gatehouses and flanking towers of its own, those of the later phase of the 1280s being semi-polygons rising from square bases with tall triangular spurs. One inner gatehouse formed a self-contained fortress residence for the castle constable. The other faced an outer court away from the dam. One side of the court contains a long hall to which was later added a huge D-shaped tower containing the a suite of private rooms over a vaulted kitchen.

The de Clare earls of Gloucester and lords of Glamorgan remained in the forefront of castle building in South Wales until the last of them was killed fighting the Scots in 1314. Apart from their small garrison posts at Castell Coch and Llantrisant, already mentioned, and a vanished castle at Treoda (Whitchurch), they had another castle at Llangwnwyd, where there are remains of a twin-towered gatehouse similar to the eastern main gatehouse at Caerphilly. They also improved their main seat at Cardiff, adding a gatehouse and hall block to the older shell keep on the motte. Their huge new castle at Morlais begun in c1287 had several round towers, including two of great size that functioned as keeps. It seems to have been left incomplete after a row with their de Bohun neighbours, and other castles begun in the early 14th century at Llanblethian and Llangibby were also left incomplete. Llangibby has a twin-towered gatehouse bigger than that at Caerphilly, plus a solar tower of composite plan, and other D-shaped towers. The one naturally weak site at Llanblethian has corner towers (one a square solar block), and a central gatehouse with polygonal-fronted towers.

In the 1250s and 60s White Castle was strengthened by adding an outer court with towers and a gatehouse, and the inner ward was given six round towers, two being placed as a pair to flank the gatehouse. The palace of the bishop of Llandaff beside his cathedral has a rectangular court with a twin-towered gatehouse with semi-octagonal fronts. At Chepstow between 1272 and 1300 Roger Bigod, Earl of Norfolk completed the task of raising the keep by one storey begun in the 1220s, built a fine new domestic suite, added the large self-contained U-shaped tower overlooking the approach, and walled in the town. At Abergavenny a rebuilding of the whole castle with curtain walls, hall and solar-tower begun in the 1290s by Lord Hastings was also in conjunction with the walling of the town. The Earl of Norfolk also built a hunting seat with at least two towers at Troggy.

The keep at Chepstow

Martin's Tower, Chepstow

Gatehouse and Marten's Tower, Chepstow

There is much work of c1260-1300 in the castles of Gower. The de Braose lords added a new block with a hall and solar in the outer ward at Swansea, whilst Oystermouth was given a new curtain wall with a twin-towered gatehouse at one acute angle, and they later added an impressive block containing a chapel on the top storey. One of their knights built a much more modest curtain wall and twin-towered gatehouse at Pennard, and at Penrice another knight added a gatehouse of unusual plan with a square block within the court and two square towers facing the field. By 1300 a new hall block with chamber wings at either end had also been added. Early 14th century work in Gower castles includes the tower at Loughor, a tower house and hall block at Weobley and a fine new chapel block at Oystermouth, whilst the remarkable arcaded parapets at Swansea are mid 14th century.

In the early 14th century a castle at St Donats was remodelled and given a closely surrounding outer ward, making it concentric, with inner and outer gatehouses. Only a fragment of a probable former courtyard castle remains in a later farmhouse at St Georges, and even the site of Aberafan Castle has now vanished. Ogmore has a 14th century courthouse and another once stood at Cardiff. Apartments at Caerphilly were remodelled in the 1320s and also of that period are extra suite of rooms at Oystermouth and Grosmont. A large rectangular gatehouse was built at Caldicot, and the principal apartments at Coity and Usk were rebuilt during the 1330s. By the late 14th century both of these castles had stone walled outer courts with their own gatehouses and towers. Caldicot has a postern tower and probably two lengths of curtain walling of the 1380s, and of about the same period is the castle at Newport which had a rectangular court with three very impressive towers, two of them octagonal, with adjacent apartments, facing the river. Because of the very high cost of the stone blocks needed to create their corners, polygonal towers are uncommon, but there is also one of the 15th century at Cardiff, a whole series of that period at Raglan, whilst polygonal bow-fronted gatehouse towers of c1285 and c1310 respectively at Llandaff and Llanblethian have already been noted, and also the towers of this shape from the 1280s on the north dam at Caerphilly.

SE tower at Newport Castle

St Donat's Castle, Glamorgan

Despite the Welsh defeats of the 1270s and the death of Llywelyn ap Gruffydd in 1282, South Wales remained a turbulent place where lordly residences needed to be capable of resisting at least a raid, if not a lengthy siege. Several castles were damaged in the Welsh uprisings of 1294, 1314 and 1316, and all the castles of the lordship of Glamorgan were captured during the Marcher lords' campaign of 1321 against the hated Despensers (favourites of Edward II), and all of them were stripped of their doors and other fittings. A small hall block in conjunction with a gateway was added in the 14th century at the small castle of Penhow. A similar block was added c1325 to two older ranges at Barry. The Old Hall at North Cornelly retains one much altered range with a gateway out of three blocks set around a small court. Candleston has a small tower and hall on one side of a modest court, two walls remain of a tower at Llanmaes and there are much-altered towers incorporated in later houses at Kemys and Tythegston. The much altered tower and remains of a court at Llandough are probably early 15th century, whilst Trecastell has remains of a walled court either of 13th or 14th century date. Some of these buildings had shooting slits in their parapets but no other defensive features. The courts had simple entrances closed only by drawbridges except for Barry, where the gateway retains a portcullis groove.

In the Vale of Glamorgan and in some of the river valleys in Gwent are quadrangular platforms with surrounding wet moats which are the sites of 13th and 14th century manor houses and hunting lodges. In most cases the original internal buildings were of perishable materials but there are traces of a stone hall within the Horseland moat at Llantryyd, footings of others have been found by excavation at Highland and Hen Gwrt (where there was a thick outer wall), and at Coity Upper the moat itself was stone lined. Moats were not necessarily defensive. They were status symbols as only the gentry could afford to create them, and were valued as a habitat for fish, eels, and water fowl, which together formed a large part of the medieval diet. They would serve as barriers to keep out wild animals and vagrants and to keep in, or restrict the movements of domestic animals and members of the household.

White Castle, Gwent

By 1403, when Owain Glyndwr led the Welsh in a rebellion that lasted several years, during which several castles were captured and damaged, many of the older castles were in a state of decay. In the later medieval period some passed to absentee landlords, and several in Gwent had become part of the duchy of Lancaster merged with the Crown in 1399. During the crisis these castles were repaired and garrisoned, but were neglected again when the danger passed. The Beauchamps, now lords of Glamorgan, rebuilt the apartments at Cardiff, whilst another branch of that family added the gatehouse at Abergavenny. For a while, at least, the Mowbrays kept Chepstow, Oystermouth and Swansea in repair without making alterations of importance. The Stradlings erected new apartments at St Donats, and the Earl of Stafford, later created Duke of Buckingham, altered and completed the unfinished castle at Newport. Sir William ap Herbert, created Earl of Worcester in 1468, was then the effective ruler of South Wales, and the most important surviving 15th century castle works in South Wales are at his seat at Raglan. The castle there has a hall central block with a court lined with apartments on one side and a service court on the other, the work being embellished with a machicolated twin-towered gateway and several towers, including a detached tower with its own wet moat containing the lordly apartments. The towers and turrets mostly have an unusual hexagonal form.

Until the 15th century glass was uncommon in secular buildings and windows were closed with shutters so that the rooms would be dark when the weather was too cold or wet for them to be opened. From the 13th century onwards window embrasures of living rooms often have stone seats. Wooden furnishings were sparse. Great lords tended to circulate from one castle or manor to another, consuming local agricultural produce on the spot and administering their manorial courts. They were also often away at the royal court or on military or diplomatic service. Their servants and some transportable furnishings went with them, leaving only caretakers in residence except when troubled times necessitated the expense of a permanent garrison. Chambers were usually plastered inside and the walls painted with allegorical or biblical scenes. Outside walls might be plastered too, and White Castle obtained its name because of it. Originally there was little privacy and many household members slept together in the hall or even in their place of work, but in the later medieval period castles were provided with ranges of lodgings so that all the main family members and household officials had their own rooms. Caldicot has fireplaces in the curtain walls for long vanished timber-framed ranges of this type.

Raglan was the last true castle built in South Wales and even there the gunports and machicolations were status symbols, arranged more with symmetry and show in mind than for their defensive usefulness. The tradition of defensive features died hard, however. The 16th century mansions of Oxwich and Pencoed are massively walled stronghouses. Oxwich has a machicolation over its gateway and both had courts with walkways on the thick enclosing walls, as did Old Beaupre, a mansion dating as late as the 1580s, although incorporating parts of a 13th and 14th century house. Another house of that period at St Fagans retained part of a 13th century courtyard castle as its forecourt, again still with walkways on the walls.

In 1536 Henry VIII abolished the independent marcher lordships, Gwent becoming the county of Monmouth, and Morgannwg, Senghenydd and Gower becoming the county of Glamorgan, an arrangement which lasted until 1974. Glamorgan was then split into three parts similar to its ancient three divisions, and Monmouthshire reverted to the name Gwent until further changes were made in 1996. When John Leland visited South Wales in the 1530s he found many of the older castles ruinous except for a hall, tower or gatehouse still maintained as a prison or courthouse.

During the 16th and early 17th centuries the Herbert Earls of Worcester remained pre-eminent in South Wales, and a branch of the family also owning several castles became Earls of Pembroke in the 1550s. They obtained further honours for their support of Charles I in the Civil War when Raglan formed one of the chief Royalist bases and was only surrendered in August 1646 after the king's cause was hopelessly lost. It was then slighted by Parliament along with other castles at Abergavenny, Llangibby, Monmouth, and probably also Caerphilly and Oystermouth. Cardiff and Chepstow also played a part in the war but both remained in use, although Chepstow required a lot of strengthening and rebuilding after its outer wall was breached during a siege in 1648. The owners of Beaupre and St Donats were heavily fined for supporting the king and their seats, although not slighted, soon fell into decay, although the latter was subsequently restored. Beaupre was downgraded to a farm with only about a third of it still roofed. Oxwich and Pencoed were also eventually abandoned, although one range at Oxwich is still roofed and there was an abortive early 20th century attempt to restore Pencoed, which is partly roofed, but is without safe upper floors. Cardiff also remains habitable although the roofed parts were considerably altered in the 18th and 19th centuries. Parts of Caldicot and Caerphilly have also been restored whilst Castell Coch has a remarkable Victorian folly grafted onto the medieval ruins. Fonmon became a mansion and escaped dereliction and Penhow remained in use as a farm until a restoration in the 1970s. An outer gatehouse at Usk forms part of a house, as do the towers at Llandough and Tythegston, and the surviving south range at North Cornelly. The other castles all now lie in ruins, although quite a number have been conserved for safe public access.

Oystermouth Castle

GAZETTEER OF CASTLES IN GWENT

ABERGAVENNY CASTLE   SO 299139   F

Hamelin de Ballon established the town and a motte and bailey castle together c1088. The castle may have had a rectangular stone keep by 1175, when Henry, third son of de Ballon's nephew, was killed by the local Welsh chieftain Sitsilt ap Dyfnwal. Abergavenny then passed via an heiress named Bertha to her husband William de Braose. He enticed Sitsilt into the castle, had him murdered, and then made a raid upon Sitsilt's base, during which one of Sitsilt's sons was killed. In 1182 Sitsilt's surviving sons took revenge by storming the castle, having filled in part of the moat with brushwood. A few of the castle garrison escaped death or capture by holding out in the keep, which remained untaken. De Braose later fell out with King John, who had William's wife Maud and son William starved to death in Windsor Castle. Another son, Reginald, joined the rebellion of Llywelyn ab Iorwerth in 1215, and repossessed Abergavenny by force. His son William supported Henry III but was captured by Llywelyn. The prisoner was treated honourably to start with, but was executed after he contrived to have an affair with Llywelyn's wife Joan. In 1233 the castle was captured by Richard Marshal during his rebellion against Henry III.

The heiress Eva de Braose married William de Cantilupe. During the minority of their son Abergavenny was held by Prince Edward. In 1273 it passed via another heiress to Henry, Lord Hastings. His grandson Lawrence was created Earl of Pembroke and died in the castle 1348. On the death of the last Lord Hastings in 1389 the castle passed to the Beauchamps. In 1402 there was a riot when the castle constable tried to hang three popular townsmen outside the castle gateway. The townsfolk stormed the castle, freed the prisoners and imprisoned the Lady Joan Beauchamp in the keep. Richard Beauchamp was killed fighting the French in 1420, leaving a daughter Elizabeth who married Sir Edward Neville. He was summed to the Parliament of 1450 as Baron Neville of Abergavenny, although it seems that the Beauchamps may have retained possession of the castle. It was held from 1495 to 1507 by Jasper Tudor, Earl of Pembroke, but later reversed to the Nevilles. The castle was described as ruined in 1645, but it must have held Royalist garrison since in 1647 Parliament decided to have it dismantled. In 1819 the Earl of Abergavenny raised a folly tower upon the foundations of the keep to provide accommodation during the shooting season. This building now forms a museum.

Two views of the double towers on the west side of Abergavenny Castle

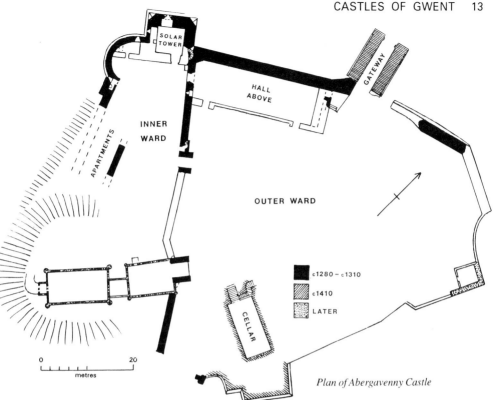

Plan of Abergavenny Castle

The castle lies on a promontory at the SW corner of the town. Nothing now remains of the town walls thought to have been begun in 1295. The keep, now replaced by the shooting box, stood on a mound at the southern apex of the site. An inner ward 20m wide extended 45m north of the keep, and east of both parts was an outer ward up to 60m across within walls 2.3m thick. The wall dividing the wards is 1.6m thick and has the lower part of a gatehouse with minimal defences. It appears that this wall was essentially to give privacy and basic security to the private apartments ranged along the west side of the inner ward rather than as a serious defensive work. The most impressive part is the double tower arrangement at the inner ward north end which is thought to be the work of John, 1st Lord Hastings, who died in 1313, and who built much of what remains of the castle. A thinly walled semicircular tower adjoins a tower with chamfered-off external corners rising by means of spurs from a base 10m square above the plinth. This tower contained a basement and three upper residential rooms reached by a spiral stair on the east side. After the fracas of 1402 the Beauchamps strengthened the weak gateway by adding in front of it a gatehouse 8m wide by 12m long. It contained a fine upper room for the constable over a long passage closed only by a two-leaved door at the outer end. The range extending west from the gatehouse to meet up with the tower with the spurs contained a hall 8m wide over a low basement. The hall was lightened by windows in the now-destroyed south wall and was 28m long, although a solar may have been divided off at the west end. On the south side of the outer wall are retaining walls forming the base of another early 15th century rectangular tower, backing onto which is an impressive vaulted cellar below courtyard level.

CAERLEON CASTLE   ST 342905   V

The castle is mentioned in Domesday Book of 1086, Caradoc ap Gryffydd or his son Owain having raised a motte over a detached bath-house between the SE corner of the Roman legionary fortress of Isca and the River Usk, whilst a bailey was laid out to the west. Henry II had the defences repaired or improved in 1171-5. Giraldus Cambrensis mentions a huge tower here, thought to have been a shell keep which finally collapsed in 1739. The castle was captured by the Welsh in 1217 but was shortly afterwards taken from Morgan ap Hywell by William Marshal, Earl of Pembroke. The round tower beside the Hanbury Arms pub 180m west of the motte is thought to have been erected by him as part of an outer bailey. It has three arrow-slits similar to those in the Garrison Tower at Usk. The blocked arch low down was cut through in the 17th century so that barrels could be brought from the river into the tower basement. The twin-towered gateway of which traced have been found at the foot of the mound are also thought to be William Marshal's work. The high embattled wall facing the road at the foot of the motte dates only from the 1840s.

Last remaining tower of Caerleon Castle

CAERWENT CASTLE   ST 471903

The small 5m high motte raised over the SE corner of the wall of the Roman town may be the Castell Gwent mentioned in a mid 12th century document. The de Lucy family held Caerwent from the 12th to the 14th century. It does not appear that the Roman defences were then complete enough to form any form of fortification.

Motte and Roman wall at Caerwent

CALDICOT CASTLE   ST 487885   O

An earth and timber castle is thought to have been built here by Walter Fitz-Roger, who died in 1127 and may have been an illegitimate son of William Fitz-Osbern's son Roger, who fled into exile in 1074. It was later held by Miles of Gloucester, Earl of Hereford, and in 1158 passed via his daughter Margaret to Humphrey de Bohun. His grandson Henry, d1220, probably built the keep during his last few years, and the bailey walls added by Henry's son Humphrey, d1275, who was created Earl of Hereford. Another Humphrey de Bohun (tenth in a sequence with this name), d1361, is thought to have added the gatehouse on the south side. In 1383 Edward III's youngest son Thomas of Woodstock obtained Caldicot by marriage to the 10 year old heiress Alianore de Bohun. The construction of the Woodstock tower on the north side of the castle is described in his accounts for 1385, and a loose stone from a destroyed building now lying in the gatehouse upper room has the initial of his wife. Thomas was created Duke of Gloucester by his nephew Richard II but was executed by him in 1396. The castle was later held by the Stafford Dukes of Buckingham, and after the 3rd Duke was executed by Henry VIII in 1521 it became part of the Duchy of Lancaster merged with the Crown. The Duchy leased the castle to the Earls of Worcester, and to the Pontypool industrialist Capel Hanbury in the mid 18th century. After holding it on a lease for some years the Lewis family purchased the ruined castle, but in 1885 they sold it to the lawyer and antiquary J.R.Cobb. He made the gatehouse, keep and two other towers habitable. His descendants sold the castle to Chepstow Rural District Council in 1963, and it now forms the centre of a country park managed by Monmouthshire County Council.

The castle has an almost intact circuit of walls and a dry encircling moat around an egg-shaped bailey 100m long by 66m wide. On a small mound at the NW corner is an ashlar-faced circular tower keep 10.6m in diameter. As tower keeps go this one is fairly low, being about 13m high. Steps lead up to a doorway into a room with four loops, from which a stair curves down in the wall to a dark and low basement buried in the mound. The basement has access via a trap-door to a deep pit-prison within the foot of an otherwise solid semi-circular turret facing west. The circular keeps of the same period (c1220) at Skenfrith and Chartley also have projecting turrets used to contain spiral stairs. In this keep there is a spiral stair in the main wall thickness rising from the entrance hall to an upper chamber and then to the roof. The upper chamber has windows with seats facing south and north (with a latrine off the latter), two west facing loops, and a fireplace. The battlements have holes for the horizontal posts for hoarding. Some of the crenels are blocked and it seems that it was intended to add an extra room at this level, where the turret contains a big vaulted recess and then has battlements (again with holes for hoarding) at a higher level.

The south front of Caldicot Castle

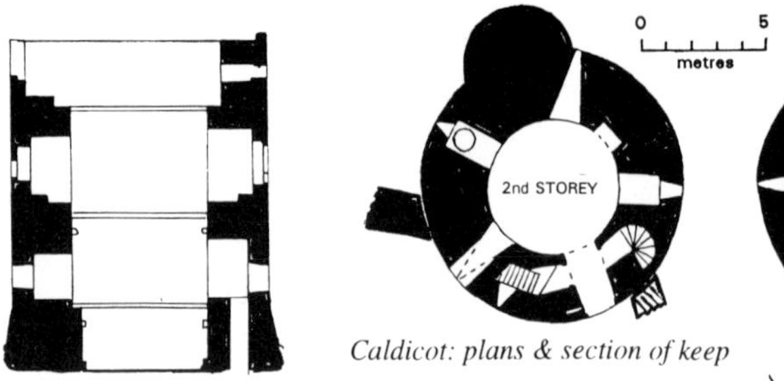

0
5
metres
2nd STOREY
3rd STOREY
Caldicot: plans & section of keep

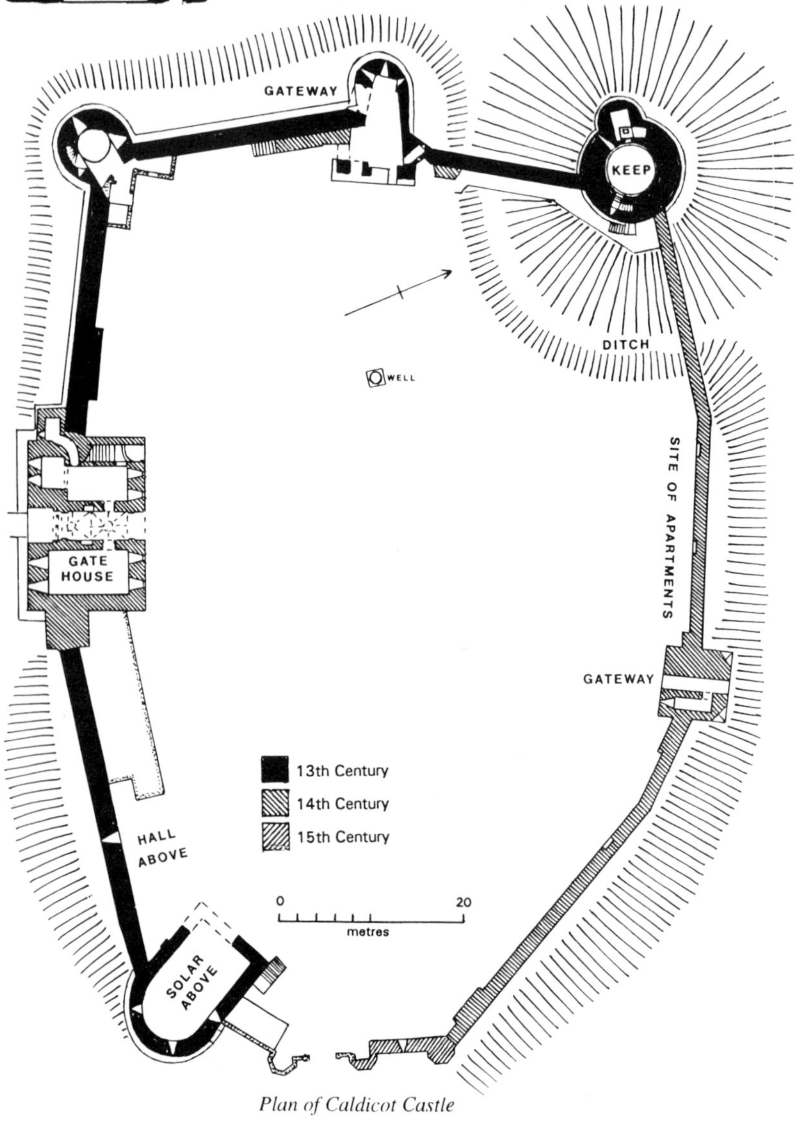

GATEWAY
KEEP
DITCH
WELL
SITE OF APARTMENTS
GATEWAY
GATE HOUSE
13th Century
14th Century
15th Century
HALL ABOVE
0
20
metres
SOLAR ABOVE
Plan of Caldicot Castle

Gateway at Caldicot

The Keep at Caldicot

The SW tower is 7.2m in diameter and has two storeys connected by a stair curving round in the wall. Towards the court the tower has adjuncts of the 1890s when it was restored from ruin. The two lengths of walling between it and the keep, and the U-shaped tower between them are probably just slightly later, the tower having a moulding at the top of its steeped base. This tower contains the unusual feature (although there is something similar at Pembroke) of a gateway in a sidewall, i.e. not facing directly out towards the field as usual. The gateway was closed by a portcullis and must have been reached by a angled timber bridge across the moat, an awkward arrangement. There was just one large room above it. In the mid 14th century this gateway was related to being a postern when a new rectangular ashlar-faced gatehouse was built in the middle of the south side of the bailey in the mid 14th century. This gateway has guardrooms flanking a vaulted central passage with a portcullis groove and murder holes. A stair in the west wall leads up to a single upper room with windows on both sides in projecting frames, a very unusual feature. The guard room windows have ogival-trefoiled heads in rectangular frames. In the re-entrant angles between the main building and the curtain walls are square latrine turrets rising one stage higher than the rest of the building.

The Woodstock Tower at Caldicot   *The west gateway at Caldicot*

The curtain wall east of the gatehouse was mostly rebuilt in the early 14th century and has several windows with foiled lights and transoms which are thought to have lighted an upper-floor hall. Beyond, at the SE corner, is a U-shaped tower 10m wide by 15.6m long which contained a solar leading off the hall over a basement. The solar has a large fireplace (now lacking its hood) and three windows facing the field with cross-loops squeezed in underneath between the seats. Just north of the tower is a breach in the medieval defences filled by a modern turret and gateway, beyond which are traces of a late 14th century building with polygonal turrets. The curtain walls around the north and NE sides of the bailey are only 1.4m thick and may be contemporary with the Woodstock Tower of the 1380s, especially since they contain three fireplaces for vanished (probably timber-framed) ranges of apartments. The ashlar-faced Woodstock tower is nearly square, 7.8m by 7.3m at the base, where it contains a postern gateway with a portcullis groove. The outer corners are chamfered off above, with spurs down to the base. A separate doorway leads onto a spiral stair in the SW corner connecting three upper rooms, each with a window at each end, a latrine on one side and a fireplace on the other. The parapet was rebuilt in the 1890s but the machicolations on the northern side are original.

Remains of keep at Castell Meredydd

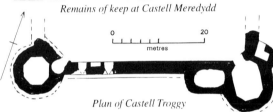

Plan of Castell Troggy

Castell Troggy

CASTELL MEREDYDD   ST 226887

In the early 13th century this site was used as a retreat by Morgan ap Hywell after he had lost his main stronghold at Caerleon to the Normans. Morgan probably built the circular tower but the bailey curtain wall was perhaps added in 1236 by Gilbert Marshal, Earl of Pembroke, after he captured the castle and held it for a short while. The site takes its name from Morgan's grandson Maredudd, to whom it passed in 1248. The bailey was about 60m square and was overlooked by higher ground to the north, on which side its defences have vanished. Slight traces of the wall footings and parts of the ditches remain on the north and on the south, where there are indications of a rhomboidal shaped building. The southern side is a cliff edge from which rise two tree-clad knobs of rock which bear the last traces of a rectangular hall block and (at the SE corner) a circular tower 8.6m in diameter over walls 2.5m thick with a latrine chute discharging down the cliff edge.

CASTELL TROGGY   ST 415952

A vegetation-obscured, ashlar-faced curtain wall 2.7m thick above a battered plinth remains on the south side of a court 40m by 30m. The fireplace and two window embrasures probably served an upper floor hall. At each end are defaced remains of a tower with an octagonal interior up to 6m in diameter. The SW tower has traces of a staircase and the SE tower (which seems to have been circular externally) has a big cess-pit beside the stub of the lost east curtain and a rectangular projection set alongside the south curtain. Begun probably c1300 by Roger Bigod III, Earl of Norfolk as a hunting seat, work on the building must have slowed down after he got into financial difficulties in 1302, leaving it incomplete at his death in 1307.

CHEPSTOW CASTLE   ST 534942   C

Domesday Book tells us that this castle was built by William Fitz-Osbern, created Earl of Hereford in 1067. The rocky ridge overlooking a cliff above the Wye offered a good defensive position which could be supplied by sea from Bristol in the event of it being blockaded by the Welsh. The site was not very suited to the creation of earthworks (the only ditch is that beyond the upper bailey) and it is generally accepted that the central rectangular keep and the curtain walls of the upper and middle baileys extending on either side of it were begun between 1067 and 1071, when William was killed fighting in France. The works had probably been completed by his son Roger of Breteuil before he rebelled against William I and fled into exile in 1075. The castle remained in royal hands until 1115, when Henry I created the lordship of Striguil for Walter Fitz-Richard, and handed over the castle to serve as its caput or main seat. Walter died heirless in 1138 and King Stephen regranted Striguil to Walter's nephew Gilbert de Clare. His son Richard, also known as Strongbow, conquered much of Ireland. At times Henry II took possession of Richard's Welsh castles when relations between them soured. The king also held the castle after Richard died in 1176, repairs being recorded in the royal Pipe Rolls for 1184-5. The heiress Isabella lived in the castle with a constable, a chaplain and his clerk, a porter and three watchmen, ten men-at-arms and ten archers, plus many servants. Another fifteen men-at-arms for defending the lordship were also based at the castle.

In 1189 Isabella married William Marshal, who was then created Earl of Pembroke. He rebuilt the east wall of the middle bailey and provided it with two round flanking towers. Later on, perhaps from 1212 until his death in 1219, he may have added lower bailey to the east with its twin-towered gatehouse. The young Henry III stayed in the castle for a few days in 1217, and in 1232 he was back at Chepstow as the guest of William's second son Richard, an elder son William having died in 1231. Richard quarrelled with the king in 1233 and was killed in Ireland in 1234. Work on building an upper storey to the keep begun by his elder brother was resumed under the third son, Gilbert, who also added the rectangular tower of the upper bailey, plus a new barbican enclosure west of that bailey. Henry III aided the works by donating oaks from the royal Forest of Dean. Gilbert was killed in a tournament in 1241 and his two younger brothers Walter and Anselm both died in 1245.

The Middle Bailey and Great Tower at Chepstow

After Anselm Marshal's death his extensive estates were divided between five sisters and their heirs. Chepstow and the southern part of the Striguil lordship passed to the eldest sister Maud, who died in 1248. Her son Roger Bigod II, Earl of Norfolk, took little interest in Chepstow as his main estates where far away in Norfolk, but his son Roger III, who succeeded in 1270, began a series of works at Chepstow. Firstly a new gatehouse was added to the west barbican, then in 1272-8 the west side of the town was enclosed with a wall, the other sides being enclosed by the river. The new halls and domestic apartments in the lower bailey were probably completed in time for Edward I visit to the castle in December 1285. A large new U-shaped tower was added to the lower ward c1286-93, and in 1292-1300 the top storey begun in the 1220s over the west end of the keep was finally completed down to the east end. Upon it was placed one of four catapults provided by Reginald the Engineer in 1298-9. The cost of this work and other extravagances put Earl Roger in debt. He resigned his estates to Edward I in 1302 in return for an annuity until his death in 1307.

Chepstow: Lower Bailey domestic buildings

In 1312 Edward II granted Chepstow to his brother Thomas, who died in 1338, leaving a second wife Mary, and a daughter Margaret, who lived until 1399. To them Chepstow was merely a source of revenue and most of the castle buildings were left to decay. From 1323 the castle was leased to Hugh Despenser the younger. He and Edward II fled to Chepstow in 1326 but there was so little support for them that the castle was surrendered to Edward's estranged consort Queen Isabella and her lover Roger Mortimer without a siege and Hugh was summarily executed. In 1399 Chepstow passed to Thomas Mowbray, Duke of Norfolk, who refortified the castle against Owain Glyndwr in 1403, installing 20 men-at-arms and 60 archery. Thomas was executed by Henry IV in 1405 but his brother John managed to obtain a fresh grant of the lordship from Henry V in 1413.

In 1468 William Herbert, Earl of Pembroke obtained Chepstow by an exchange of lands with John Mowbray's grandson John. In 1469 the two brothers of Edward IV's consort Queen Margaret took refuge in the castle but they were unpopular with the garrison and were handed over to their enemy the earl of Warwick for execution. In 1491 the second William Herbert's daughter Elizabeth succeeded to his extensive estates. She was married to Charles, an illegitimate son of Henry, Duke of Somerset, who was created Earl of Worcester. This couple updated the domestic buildings in the lower bailey and their son probably built the now-demolished range against the hall dividing the lower and middle baileys in the 1540s.

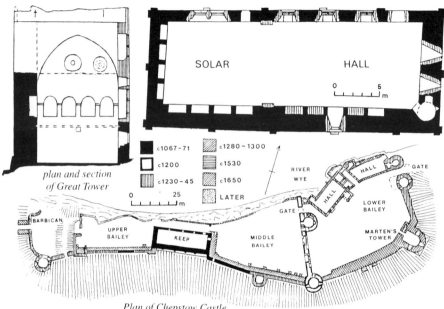

plan and section
of Great Tower

Plan of Chepstow Castle

Henry, 5th Earl of Worcester was created a marquis by Charles I. He held Chepstow for King Charles I in 1642 but when a Parliamentary force under William Waller advanced against it in 1643 the Royalists withdrew into the castle and abandoned the town. Both were garrisoned by the Royalists throughout 1644. In October 1645 the castle garrison of 64 men equipped with 17 guns and 30 horses surrendered after a short siege. Early in 1648 the castle was seized and garrisoned for King Charles by Sir Nicholas Kemys. He refused to submit to Cromwell, who left a regiment to besiege the castle whilst he marched off to take out another Royalist garrison in the castle at Pembroke. Four guns battered the castle until most of the battlements had been destroyed, making the wall-walks untenable, and a breach was opened in the wall of the lower bailey. Sir Nicholas still refused to surrender and was killed during an assault when the garrison began to issue out of the breach and surrender individually.

Parliament granted the castle to Cromwell, who had it repaired and garrisoned by a company of foot. Expenditure on it of £300 in 1650 probably refers to the rebuilding of the breached wall, the lowering of the towers and the remodelling of the parapets in a thicker form better able to withstand artillery fire. Another £500 was spent on it in 1662, when the castle was restored to Lord Herbert, and in 1663 the garrison was reduced to a half company. During the 1650s the Royalist bishop Jeremy Taylor was confined in the castle, and dduring the 1660s and 70s Henry Martin was kept in comfortable confinement in the large SE tower now bearing his name in retribution for his part in the trial and execution of Charles I.

The garrison was finally withdrawn in 1688 and in 1690 the defences were partly dismantled and the guns removed to Chester. The descendants of Henry, Marquis of Worcester, created Duke of Beaufort in 1682, continued to own the castle and the freehold rights of the town wall until in 1914 they were sold to Mr W.R.Lysaght. Parts of the castle remained roofed and inhabited until the early 19th century but were not used by the dukes. In 1943 and 1953 the town wall and castle ruins were placed in the guardianship of the State, now represented by Cadw.

The lower bailey is entered at its NE corner through a gatehouse with round towers of differing sizes. Each tower contained two upper rooms with 16th century mullioned windows set over a prison in the northern tower and a guard room in the southern one, which has lost its rectangular back containing a small room. The round-arch between the towers is now closed by a pair of modern doors but originally there were also inner and outer portcullises. The doors are replacements of originals now amongst the displayed material in the domestic block main solar. Recent tree-ring analysis indicated a late 12th century date for the original doors. This suggests the outer gatehouse could be as early as c1190, although c1212-25 would seem more likely since it is probable the lower bailey was added after the strengthening of the middle bailey. An arch suspended between the towers provided machicolations and one stump of walling remains of a barbican in the form of a narrow passageway.

At the SE corner of the lower bailey is the U-shaped Marten's Tower built in the 1280s on the site of a smaller older tower. It is a self contained structure 16.4m by 13.5m wide semi-circular externally (but semi-polygonal internally) rising from a rectangular base with spurs towards the field and having higher square turrets where the curtains adjoin it on either side. The entrance, closed by a portcullis, gives onto the second level (there was an unlit basement below it reached a trapdoor) and also the foot of a spiral stair to two pleasant upper rooms with fireplaces, arrowloops facing the field, large later windows towards the bailey and latrines on the south. Two other doorways leading out to the wall-walks on either side of the tower were also closed by portcullises, so the tower functioned as a second keep. A new high-pitched roof containing an extra room was added in the 16th century. The east turret contains an elaborate chapel at top storey level. Upon each merlon of the parapet is an ornamental figure. The curtain west of the tower is assumed to be where the breach of 1648 was made, after which it was rebuilt and thickened using materials taken from the upper parts of the Great Tower. In spite of later buttresses the wall leans outwards and has needed a series of braces built across the top recently.

The whole of the north side of the lower bailey, overlooking the river, is filled with domestic buildings of c1278-85. Behind the gatehouse north tower lay a block containing a cellar and two upper private rooms reached from the court by external timber stairs leading to south facing upper doorways. The next part to the west formed a kitchen probably with a central fire with smoke escaping through a louvre in the roof, since although there is an oven in the north wall there are no fireplaces. One blocked round-headed window shows that something still remains here of an older domestic building of c1190-1200. Beyond is a service passage reached from the court by a doorway. It has access to the kitchen and to a latrine on the cliff-edge on its east side, and on its west side there are doorways to two service rooms, between which is a set of steps rising up to the main hall between a pantry and buttery at hall level set over the two lower service rooms. There is also a stair leading down to a rib-vaulted cellar with a NW facing window. Originally this was a doorway allowing supplies to be hoisted up from boats far below but this function was later taken over by a doorway at the west end of a later balcony perched on the cliff edge and reached off the cellar steps.

The great hall measures 17m by 8.7m and has remains of two fine windows facing SE into the court. It is assumed there were once others in the now rebuilt NW wall facing the river. A stringcourse round the whole room at mid-height rose up over the openings. The hall is reached from the south through a rib-vaulted porch with a two-light transomed window and buttressed corners. One would expect a main private chamber to open off the dais end of the hall but since it lay close to the middle gateway there was only space there for two small unimportant rooms linked by a spiral stair. Instead the main chamber was placed over the pantry and buttery and was reached by a spiral stair beside the porch.

Town Gateway, Chepstow

Interior of the Great Tower at Chepstow

The middle bailey forms a triangle with the keep or Great Tower at the apex. Part of the south wall with a blocked postern near the latter is of 1067-75. The rest of the south and east walls, and the three circular towers flanking them with arrowslits, are of c1190-1200. The towers have been much altered, one having been filled up with earth in the 1650s when it and the SE tower were given new parapets suitable for artillery, whilst the northern tower protecting the pointed-arched middle gateway was later converted into a kitchen (with fireplace and oven) and the wall south of it pierced with openings for an adjacent range.

The Great Tower is a hall keep 32m long by 13m wide originally about 10m high at the west end but higher (since it rises from a lower level) further east. There are thin pilaster buttresses at the corners and also along the sides, dividing the ends into two bays and the long sides into five. The vulnerable south wall is 2.6m thick and has no original external openings, whilst the north wall is only 1.2m thick. The sloping ground allows a sub-basement 2.2m high at the east end, tailing off to nothing at the west end and entered through a doorway later pierced through the north wall. Timber steps (on the site of a ramp of the 1650s) must have led up to the east doorway with voussoirs with Xs in boxes and a semicircular tympanum. This led to a dark basement with just three small north-facing windows and onto the foot of a staircase up to the hall and the wall-walk. The top level formed a hall in the eastern three bays with a solar in the western two, the width of the building necessitating a row of central posts and beams to support the floors. The solar has four blind round-headed recesses in each of the west and south walls. In the 13th century the solar was given a large new double window in the north wall and it then became the dais end of a hall now extending the full length of the building and having only a very ornate two bay arcade (now destroyed) dividing it. This arcade supported the east wall of a new solar raised above the old one. The hall originally had five southern recesses of its own but three were blocked up and the middle one was made into a lancet window, whilst two other lancets were inserted high up in the east wall and a new doorway reached byu a timber stair was pierced in the north wall. Later in the 13th century the original hall was provided with three new north windows with plate-tracery, transoms, and seats in the embrasures, and then another room was created above it in turn, so that the whole length of the building was now heightened by about 8m. On the east and south sides these upper walls were destroyed in the 1650s to provide the material for strengthening the curtain walls.

Between the keep and the cliff edge is a narrow space only enclosed by walls in the 13th century. The openings on the north side may have led to a timber viewing gallery overhanging the cliff-edge. To the west lies the upper bailey, a rectangle 38m long by up to 16m wide. It has a thin loopholed north wall of the 1650s and a south curtain which is partly of 1067-75, and partly of c1220, but doubled in thickness in the 1650s. The material for this thickening was obtained by demolishing the inner walls facing the court of a rectangular tower at the SW corner. This tower still has round-headed windows facing south and west which lighted a fine upper room over a basement. The tower is though to have been added c1220 to provide the recently widowed Countess Isabel with her own private apartment. It must have once been accompanied by a series of other rooms, probably timber-framed, against the curtain wall. Immediately north of the tower is a gateway facing out across a ditch in which is the pier of a 16th century bridge. This ditch takes up nearly half of the internal space of a mid 13th century barbican with arrowloops in its curtain and (on three levels) in a round tower at the SW corner. In the early 1270s the originally modest gateway of the barbican was strengthened by adding a tower with battered walls. It has a passageway with three portcullis grooves. Above are two rooms, one with three crossloops facing west. Only the corbelling remains of the parapet.

A wide bend of the River Wye enclosed the town on the south and east, and the castle and river together blocked off the north side. In 1272-8 the Port Wall, 2m thick, 4.5m high to the wall-walk, and 1,150m long was built across the western side to close off an area of 130 acres, far more than the castle, town and priory together ever required in the medieval period. The thin wall which crossed the castle ditch has gone and two breaches have been made in the late 20th century for the A48 bypass and access to a car park. The SE end has also gone, pierced first by the railway in 1850 and then swept away for dockyard extensions during the First World War. The remainder survives mostly intact, although the ditch in front has been filled it. There are seven open-backed D-shaped bastions 8m in external diameter which rise slightly above the wall, the still surviving wall-walk of which is carried round them at a higher level. At the edge of the castle ditch the wall now ends in a rectangular turret. Closing off the High Street is the Town Gate, a rectangular tower of 13th century origin, although the description "New Gate" in 1487 suggests a total rebuilding, whilst the pair of worn coats of arms probably date from 1524, when the upper rooms were adapted as a prison. The battlements are a modern rebuild. Towards the west there are separate arches side-by-side for carts and pedestrians.

The west end of Chepstow Castle

The Port Wall at Chepstow

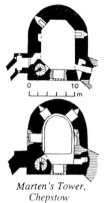

Marten's Tower, Chepstow

DINGESTOW CASTLE   SO 455104

The moated platform 65m long by 40m wide above confluence of the River Trothy and a tributary to the west is the site of a castle which was being built in 1182 by William de Braose and Ranulph le Poer, Sheriff of Hereford. The Welsh, having been antagonised by de Braose's cruelty, raided the site and killed the sheriff. Nothing remains of possible later stone defences. A motte and bailey (presumably the site of an earlier castle here) lie in woodland on the other side of the river.

DINHAM CASTLE   ST 481923

In woodland above a stream are slight and rather overgrown remains of a tower, courtyard and outbuildings begun by the Welsh family in the 13th century, perhaps on the site of a castle of 1150. The chief seat of this family was at Llanwern and Dinham was later leased to the Beauchamps, and then sold in the late 16th century to William Blethin, Bishop of Llandaff.

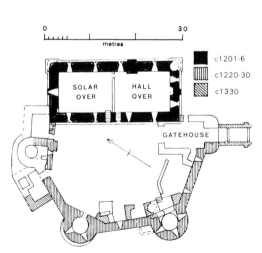

Plan of Grosmont Castle

Grosmont Castle

GROSMONT CASTLE   SO 406244   F

King Stephen obtained Grosmont by exchanging lands with Payn Fitz-John and a castle is first mentioned in 1154, the year of Stephen's death. It remained royal until King John granted Grosmont to Hubert de Burgh in 1201. The room erected in 1185 and the storehouse building during the administration of the place by the sheriffs of Hereford must have been of wood. Hubert erected a hall block on the east side of the large but low motte before falling out of favour, Grosmont being held by William de Braose in 1206. The curtain wall with a rectangular gatehouse and three circular towers completing the circuit of stone defences on the motte were erected between 1219, when Hubert recovered Grosmont, and 1232, when he fell out of favour with Henry III. In 1227 the king had granted Hubert fifty oaks towards the building work at Grosmont, In 1233 King Henry's army, encamped outside the castle in the following year, was defeated in a surprise night attack by Richard Marshal, who took several prisoners but did not capture the castle. De Burgh died in 1243 and in 1254 Henry III granted the castle to Prince Edward. However in 1267 it was transferred to Henry's younger son Edmund, Earl of Lancaster. His son Thomas was executed for rebellion against Edward II in 1322 but a younger son, Henry, was later restored to the earldom and in the 1330s he improved the accommodation at Grosmont, modifying the SW tower replacing the north tower by a new range. The castle probably saw little use after John of Gaunt married Henry's granddaughter Blanche in 1361. It withstood a siege by Owain Glyndwr in 1405, when it was relieved by Prince Henry, later Henry V. The castle was abandoned by the early 16th century and a survey of 1563 noted that all the "Tymber, iron and lead is rotten or taken away". The ruin was sold by the Duchy of Lancaster to the Duke of Beaufort in 1825, and in 1902 it was again sold to the antiquary Joseph Bradney. It passed into State care in 1923 (now Cadw).

The hall block at Grosmont Castle

SW tower at Grosmont Castle

Tower at Kemys Manor

Kemys Manor: tower plans

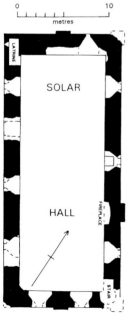

The hall block at Grosmont

The castle consists of a low but deeply ditched motte covered in stone buildings and a small bailey to the south where there are traces of a ditch but no signs of buildings, although stone footings for a probably timber-framed barn or stable have been reported. The motte summit may have been circular originally but is now D-shaped with a hall block of 1201-4 on the east side and a stone-walled court of the 1220s extending 20m to the west. The hall block is 29m long by 13m wide over walls 2.2m thick above a battered plinth. The pilaster buttresses clasping the NE corner and the SE corner (which contained a spiral staircase between the levels) are mostly broken down. Other pilasters strengthened the walls behind where there were fireplaces. The block contained a hall with a much smaller chamber divided off at the north end, and two lower rooms, at least one of which was habitable since it had a fireplace in the south end wall. The hall had a fireplace on the east side and the chamber a fireplace at the north end, plus a latrine in the NW corner. The upper windows were originally lancets in deep embrasures but all of them, and the hall doorway formerly reached by wooden steps, have lost all their dressed stonework. The lower rooms were more equal in size, were lighted by small loops and were entered by two doorways set on either side of a crosswall.

Adjoining the SW corner of the hall was the gatehouse, a block 13.3m long by 8.2m wide with rounded corners facing the field, and now mostly reduced to its base. The drawbridge was flanked by a thinly walled barbican. Where the 1.8m thick south curtain adjoined there was a staircase to the two upper storeys. The SW and NW towers are both about 8m in external diameter, and originally had a dark basement and three upper levels with narrow slits. In the 1330s the SW tower was extended 2.5m towards the court and spiral stairs were provided to the upper rooms, where the loops were enlarged and fireplaces were provided, whilst further up there are windows towards the court in the extension. A fifth storey was also added. The wall-walk between the towers survives and has been made accessible for visitors. The piers backing against the wall here must have supported some sort of gallery. Between the gatehouse and the SW tower was a timber framed building, perhaps a kitchen. Only the base remains of the outer part of the north tower, which was later incorporated into a block of extra apartments. The outer parts are now lost but the original south end wall of the tower, heightened and extended to the east in the 1330s and surmounted by an octagonal chimney, still stand high. Shortly afterwards another three storey block was added to the west. This is also now much ruined but a pit can be seen in the base of its north wall.

KEMYS MOTTE & MANOR   ST 389939 & 390940

A footpath from the carpark and toilets beside the A449 leads down to a small but fine 5m high motte squeezed into the less than 25m width between a minor road and a steep drop to the River Usk (see plan on page 4). A 3m high rampart shields the tiny bailey from the higher ground. The house to the east has a 13th century tower 7.5m square with a late 16th century extension to the south, there being a west porch at the junction of the parts, adjoining which is an annex containing a straight flight of stairs. A blocked opening marks a former projecting latrine from the tower second storey SW corner. There are stairs in the tower south wall. The third storey has another stair truncated when the whole building was given a new hipped roof in the late 17th century and another wing added to the SE. Not long afterwards the Kemys family, who had lived here since the early 13th century. sold the estate.

LLANFAIR DISCOED CASTLE   ST 446923

In the grounds of a house west of the church are overgrown fragments of a small courtyard castle probably built by Sir Ralph Monthermer on a site perhaps previously occupied by the Fitz-Payns descended from Payn Fitz-John. In the late 14th century the castle passed to the Montacutes. It reverted to the Crown in 1541 after the execution of Margaret, wife of Sir Richard Pole. James I sold it to Edward Woodward in 1610, and he in turn sold it to Rhys Kemeys. At the SE corner a circular tower stands high and adjoins a curtain wall pierced by defaced openings for an important room. There is a smaller tower at the SW corner and then a wall runs north to where one of a pair of gate-towers still remains. There is also one high piece of the east curtain wall but any remains of the north side of the court are now buried under heaps of debris and thick vegetation.

Llanfair Discoed Castle

LLANGIBBY CASTLE   ST 364974 & 370974

No stone buildings now remain visible on the heavily overgrown motte near Castle Farm, but the buildings referred to in 1262 may have stood there. The estate had passed to the de Clares in 1245. There is a further mention of construction work in 1286 and we cannot be sure which site this refers to. The ruin on the tree-clad hill above (also known as Tregrug) is thought to have been begun c1312 by Gilbert de Clare and to have been left incomplete when he was killed at Bannockburn in 1314, although it is just possible that it was begun in 1322-3 by Hugh le Despenser and left incomplete in 1326 after this highly unpopular favourite of Edward II was captured and executed. In 1554 Queen Mary sold the estate to the Williams family. They supported Parliament in the Civil War, but in 1648 they had a garrison of 60 men holding the castle for King Charles, so it must have then been still defensible. The building shows evidence of slighting and the fact that they built a newer house lower down soon afterwards (demolished in 1951) suggests they may actually have inhabited it for about a century. A 17th century barn by the farmhouse of Tregrug to the north has a decayed late medieval roof said to have come from the castle, although the ruin shows no signs of any stone internal domestic buildings.

The roughly rectangular bailey 150m long by 75m wide is one of the largest single-enclosure castles in Britain. Only slight traces (with a latrine chute) remain of a twin-round towered gatehouse and another tower further west on the south side, one of the two towers on the east has vanished along with much of the wall there, and the north tower is much ruined, but the 2m thick north curtain wall otherwise still stands to its full internal height of about 6m and there are structures of great interest at the western corners. That on the SW is a huge gatehouse similar in size and plan to those at Beaumaris begun in 1295. It has two U-shaped towers flanking a long passageway which seems to have been narrowed later and no evidence of its defences remain. Circular turrets on the east corners (the SE turret projects from the south curtain wall) contain spiral stairs to the lost (or perhaps never completed) upper storeys. There are also large turret on each side to contain latrines, that on the south have an impressive pit serving a group of four, one each from two basement rooms once divided by a now destroyed crosswall, and two more from higher up.

The NW corner has a structure with a unique plan which probably formed the lord's residence. It has a rectangular block 10.4m wide with circular turrets on the east corners flanking a doorway between them with a portcullis groove. The NE turret contained a lofty vaulted room and the SE turret contains a spiral staircase. The west end is a 12m diameter circular structure set not as a half-round apse but as a three-quarter round projecting from the NW corner but without any division between its interior and that of the main structure, in a manner which resembles the relationship between the NW tower and the solar block at Goodrich in Herefordshire. This part of the building, which shows signs of movement, probably because of having been blown up in 1648, has parts remaining of rectangular latrine projections to north and south. The latter adjoins another chamber with traces of arcading and a vault where the otherwise destroyed west curtain adjoined the tower.

LLANHILLETH CASTLE   ST 219020   V

West of the hilltop church of St Illtyd is a 5m high motte lying in a farmyard. In the 1920s excavations behind the cottages east of the church revealed the now covered-over again bases of two remarkable structures representing two different periods in the 13th century. One was a tower 19m in diameter with a central pillar and the other a tower 21m square with recessed corners and a cruciform interior with round-headed loops having steeply shelving embrasures with chamfered rere-arches.

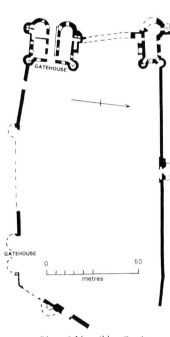

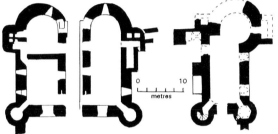

Portcullis groove in Lord's Tower at Llangibby

Plan of Llangibby Castle

Plan of Gatehouse

Plan of Lord's Tower

SW stair turret of gatehouse at Llangibby

The keep at Monmouth

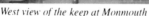

West view of the keep at Monmouth

Monmouth: bridge gateway

MONMOUTH CASTLE   SO 507129   F

Monmouth lies in the neck of a loop formed at the confluence of the Monnow and Wye. The castle and priory were founded by William Fitz-Osbern in 1067-71 and after his son Roger was dispossessed in 1075 William I granted the lordship to Wilhenoc, a Breton from Dol. The latter's nephew William Fitz Baderon held the lordship at the time of Domesday Book in 1086. His descendant John of Monmouth was defeated in 1233 by Richard Marshal, Earl of Pembroke in a battle fought near the town, after which the castle was captured. John lacked an heir and in 1256 he handed over Monmouth to Henry III's eldest son Edward in return for lands elsewhere. The castle was captured during the rebellion of Simon de Montfort, who was at Monmouth with the captured Henry III in June 1264. When Henry's younger son was created Earl of Lancaster in 1267 Monmouth was transferred to him. Edmund built the hall beside the keep, whilst c1350 his grandson Henry remodelled the hall in the keep itself. The future Henry V was born in the castle in 1387, being the grandson of Edward III's son John of Gaunt, who became Duke of Lancaster in 1362. The Lancaster estates in this part of Wales merged with the Crown when Henry's father seized the throne as Henry IV in 1399. In 1404 a band of Owain Glyndwr's supporters were defeated near Grosmont, but then managed to rout an English force in the Trothy valley and chased the remnants all the way back to Monmouth, where outlying houses were burnt.

Monmouth became a shire town in 1536 and some of the rooms in the decaying castle were kept in repair for the assize courts even after the rest of the castle was disposed of in 1630. Monmouth was a place of strategic importance during the Civil War and held a Royalist garrison until captured by a ruse in September 1644. In November Lord Charles Somerset managed to recapture it during the absence of the Parliamentary governor, Colonel Massey. Another Parliamentary force under Sir Trevor Williams of Llangibby and Colonel Morgan, Governor of Gloucester, finally captured Monmouth in October 1645. In the castle, which was undermined during the siege, they found 7 guns, 300 muskets, 600 pikes, and a good supply of ammunition and provisions. In 1647 Colonel Kyrle arrived to supervise the demolition of the castle defences. A large circular keep built by John of Monmouth c1235-40 was destroyed and later replaced by Great Castle House, an ashlar-faced four storey building dated 1673 over the doorway. It was built by Henry Somerset, who became 3rd Marquis of Somerset in 1667, President of the Council of Wales and the Marches in 1672, and 1st Duke of Beaufort in 1682. His grandson, the 2nd Duke, was born in the house in 1684. It was later used as a judges' lodging, then a girls' school, and then as the officer's mess of the Royal Monmouthshire Engineers Militia. It is now a museum, whilst the ruins of the keep and hall are conserved by Cadw.

The castle lies above the Monnow in the west corner of the walled town. It had an oval court about 100m long by 60m wide with a twin towered gatehouse begun by Henry VI in the 1440s on the east side. In c1550 a survey recommended that this now-vanished building should have its top storey completed to increase security at the castle and to provide rooms for prisoners. In 1370 there was a chapel lying close to the gateway. On the west side are remains of a 12th century hall keep 21m long by 13m wide which is thought to have contained a hall and chamber end to end over a low basement still retaining three original round-headed loops in the 1.7m thick east wall. The vulnerable west wall projecting outside the curtain wall is 3.0m thick. It but the central part of this wall has gone. The NE corner is missing and a house encroaches upon the space. The other corners have clasping buttresses and the SE corner has a spiral staircase. In the mid 14th century the upper storey was remodelled and given a new south doorway and a fine two-light east window. The keep was originally entered through a forebuilding but c1270 this was removed to make way for a second hall 18.5m by 10.5m wide internally to the south. The west wall is part of the original bailey wall and the south wall has tall blocked windows. Only the base remains, with a fireplace, of the north wall. The east end was screened off in the usual way with doorways at either end. This hall, being used for assizes, was better maintained than the rest of the castle at the time of the survey of c1550, and the five light mullion-and-transom window in the east wall is of that period.

In 1297 and 1315 the Crown authorised the collection of tolls to pay for the replacing in stone of the Norman earth and timber defences of what had original been the castle outer bailey but which had become the centre of the town. Leland, Camden and Speed's map of 1610 all agree that only the most vulnerable NE side ever had a proper stone wall. The wall ran between the twin-towered East Gate (of which one round tower remains embedded in the Old Nag's Head in Old Dixton Road) and the now-vanished now-vanished Monk's Gate closing off the road headed north to Hereford. A short section of wall also connected the West Gate across Monnow Street with the nearby southern corner of the castle. Speed indicates a fourth gate facing SE beside the head of the bridge over the Wye. The defences were described by Leland c1538 as very decayed. At the south end of Monnow Street is a survival which is unique in Britain, a medieval bridge with a gatehouse rising above the pier nearest the town. Rounded ends rise from the triangular cutwaters. The passage was closed by a portcullis and defended on the outer side by three machicolations opening from an upper room originally reached by a spiral stair on the north side, where there was a latrine. The passage and upper windows have been altered and side passages inserted for pedestrians in the 19th century. There were originally open battlements and the hipped roof is 18th century. The bridge led out to Over Monnow, a surburb of the 1170s protected with its own ditch called the Clawdd Ddu probably filled with water from the river. Part of a timber bridge of that period came to light in 1988.

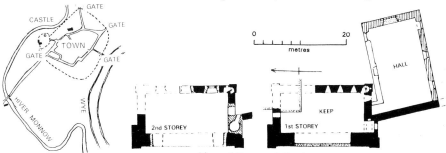

Site plan of Monmouth   *Plans of Monmouth Castle*

Newport Castle from across the River Usk.

NEWPORT CASTLE   ST 309875 & 312885   F

Robert Fitz-Hamon gave lands here to Robert of Hay, who c1100 raised a motte with a summit diameter of 15m on a commanding side south of St Woolos' church (now the cathedral). The mound was buried in spoil from a railway tunnel in the 1840s. Other references to a castle at Newport up until the 1340s probably refer to this site although they could refer to an building replaced by the existing stone castle on the west bank of the Usk to the NE. Henry II stayed in the castle in 1172, and in 1184 had it repaired after a Welsh attack, Hywell ap Iorwerth then being its custodian. King John had the castle repaired in 1207. It was captured during Richard Marshal's revolt of 1233, and it was seized by Simon de Montfort in 1265. After Gilbert de Clare's death in 1314, Hugh de Audley and Hugh le Despenser, each married to one of de Clare's sisters, both claimed Newport. Despenser repaired the castle with 300 oaks after de Audley, supported by the Bohuns and Mortimers, captured the castle after a four day siege in May 1321. Following Edward III's accession to the throne in 1327 de Audley enjoyed undisputed possession of Newport until his death in 1347.

Ralph, Earl of Stafford, married de Audley's heiress but he was busy rebuilding his castle at Stafford, and it seems more likely that it was his son Hugh, founder of the nearby Augustinian friary, who began the existing building a few years before 1386, when he set off on a pilgrimage to Jerusalem, from which he never returned. The castle seems to have remained incomplete whilst his second and third sons successively succeeded as minors, and it was still unfinished when the fourth son Edmund, who came of age in 1397, was killed at the battle of Shrewsbury in 1403. Shortly afterwards the town of Newport was laid waste by Owain Glyndwr. Accounts survive recording hasty work on the castle during the summer of 1405 in an attempt to complete the defences enough to make them tenable against the Welsh rebels.

The castle was only properly completed after Edmund's son Humphrey came of age in 1424. In 1447 there is mention of the north curtain wall being raised and pieces of Dundry stone were obtained for capping the merlons. Favoured by Henry VI, Earl Humphrey was created Duke of Buckingham in 1444, but was killed at the battle of Northampton in 1460. Henry, 2nd Duke was executed by Richard III in 1483, and Edward, 3rd Duke, was executed and attainted by Henry VIII in 1521. Newport was granted to William Herbert in 1547, but he later leased it to his cousin, another William Herbert of St Julians. Under the lease terms he carried out minor repairs but the building was ruinous by 1645. From 1820 to 1899 there was a brewery in the castle using water (said to be excellent) from the well. The ruins have been in state guardianship (now Cadw) since the 1930s.

Newport Castle

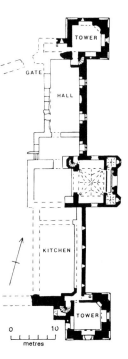

Rising beside the tidal mouth of the Usk is the impressive 50m long east front of the castle with a square tower in the middle and octagonal towers on square bases with tall spurs at the corners. The bailey extended 60m to the west, but although towers may have been planned there originally, as completed the vulnerable landward side had just a plain curtain wall and a wet moat filled from the river. The irregular layout on the north side and the eventual provision of a weak north gate on the site of where the hall porch had originally been laid out are further evidence of changes to the original plan. There seems also to have been another gate on the south side. In 1792 the west arm of the moat became part of a canal and spoil from digging other sections was dumped in the north and south arms of the moat. The whole of the western part of the bailey has now vanished under a complex of roads.

The two rooms in the NE tower (where one late 16th century window remains) are linked by a stair in a turret projecting into the hall NW corner and had latrines on the west side. The rooms probably served the lordship steward and the room over the gate would have been used for the manorial records. The hall inner wall is destroyed to its base but a pair of two-light windows with embrasure seats and a fireplace remain in the east curtain wall. A chamber at the south end may have originally served at the solar but after remodelling in the 1430s it became an ante-room to an audience chamber west of the middle tower. An arch opened from this space into a fine tierceron-vaulted space in the tower itself where the duke would have sat. Behind the duke's throne was a passage connecting closets in polygonal turrets facing east and containing machinery for a portcullis closing off a dock for a small ship below. A spiral stair on the north side led to another room above, now very ruined, which may have been a chapel. A gallery within the thickness of the southern section of the east curtain connected these rooms with a suite of three rooms for the duke's own private use in the SE tower. The rooms have fireplaces and access to latrines, and they are linked by a spiral stair on the west side. All their windows are 15th century modifications. The top room has eight corbels for a pointed roof. Against the curtain wall lay the kitchen, a large oven being discovered here in 1858.

The town had at least three 14th century gates, two of which partly survived in 1799. The Westgate Hotel stands on the site of a structure similar to the middle tower of the castle which bore the Stafford arms. There is doubt as to whether there was a stone wall, but there was a ditch, rampart and palisade by the 12th century.

PENCOED CASTLE   ST 406894   V

The castle consists of a court about 35m square with the east side closed by a roofed but derelict range of apartments, the south side has a curtain wall 1.6m thick but now only about 2.5m high and the west side has a ruined central square gatehouse connected by a curtain wall to a ruined circular SW tower 5m in diameter. North of the gatehouse are traces of a range, and extending across towards it from the main range (with which it makes an acute angle) was a north range of which only a high fragment of the south wall now remains, with one late 15th century window. This part is thought to be the work of Sir Thomas Morgan, who held Pencoed from 1480 to 1510, whilst the gatehouse and east range are assumed to have been built by his grandson, another Sir Thomas, between 1542 and 1565. The circular tower is said to be a relic of the house Sir Richard de la More had here in 1270, although all its doorways and windows are clearly of c1500 and the curtain walls could also be that late. The tower contained two low rooms linked by a stair under a brick vault and a third room above reached from the now broken down wall-walk of the west curtain wall. The gatehouse has an undefended passage with a partly broken down vault and contains windows with arched lights under square labels which are reported to have had heraldic glass including the arms of the 2nd Sir Thomas and his father Sir William. Towards the field the gatehouse has two turrets with their outer angles chamfered off. The SW turret contains a spiral stair and the NW turret the latrines.

The east range is faced with very fine ashlar and has a central porch giving access to a lofty ground floor hall, above which is the great chamber, reached by a wide scale-and-platt staircase in a projection on the east side. South of the hall is a slightly later wing containing a parlour with a four-light south window and two pairs of upper rooms over a cellar. North of the hall the range has three storeys linked by another stair at the north end. Adjoining the hall is a chapel with a piscina, and beyond is the kitchen with a huge fireplace with an oak lintel in the north wall, perhaps part of the late 15th century mansion. To the NE is a 16th century dovecote. After the last Morgan sold the estate in 1701 the castle passed to the Gwynns of Llanhowell who farmed the lands but allowed the building to decay. In 1914 it was purchased by Lord Rhondda and by the time of his death in 1918 the east range had been mostly restored and provided with a new embattled parapet, but a new house was built on the north in 1922 and the old building allowed to decay again.

East range of Pencoed Castle

East range, Pencoed

Gatehouse at Pencoed Castle

Corner tower at Pencoed

Old print of Pencoed Castle

PENHOW CASTLE   ST 425908   O

Roger de Seymour (originally spelt Sancto Mauro), who witnessed a charter of a gift to Monmouth Priory in 1129, perhaps had his seat at Castell Pren Wood near Parc Seymour. By 1200 one of his descendants had built a small rectangular tower keep on the present site. The small court east of it was probably given a stone curtain wall by Sir William Seymour in the 1230s, although the first specific mention of the castle is not until 1306. The hall block on the south side was probably built by Roger Seymour in the late 14th century. Jane Seymour, who married Henry VIII in 1536, and who died the following year after giving birth to the future Edward VI, was descended from Roger's uncle Roger, who inherited the adjacent manor of Udny as a younger son. Early in the 15th century Penhow passed to John Bowles, spouse of the heiress Isabella Seymour. Their grandson Sir Thomas Bowles, who married Maud Morgan of Pencoed in 1482, and was knighted at Berwick the same year, rebuilt the outer wall of the hall block, placing the Seymour, Bowles and Morgan arms on one of the label stops of a three-light window lighting the hall. In the mid 16th century the castle passed to Sir George Somerset, 3rd son of the Earl of Worcester.

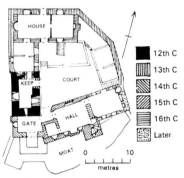

Key:
- 12th C
- 13th C
- 14th C
- 15th C
- 16th C
- Later

Plan of Penhow Castle

Sir Henry Billingsley, High Sheriff of Monmouthshire in 1599, may have built the present L-shaped house in the NE corner of the court, but its features are mostly of the time of Thomas Lewis of St Pierre, who purchased the castle in 1674, whilst the sash windows were inserted by the Lloyd family, who purchased the castle in 1714 and held it until the 19th century. From 1709 until 1966 the castle was a tenanted farm and gradually fell into a very decayed state. In 1973 Stephen Weeks became the owner and restoration was begun. Excavations then rediscovered the rock-cut moat on the south side and the drawbridge arrangements.

Penhow Castle from the south

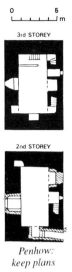

0 5 m

3rd STOREY

2nd STOREY

*Penhow:
keep plans*

Penhow Castle from the west

The castle lies on top of a small hill and had stables and other outbuildings in an undefended outer court extending towards the church. The inner court is D-shaped with a tower keep just 9.7m long by 6.4m wide lying in the middle of the 27m long straight west side. The pointed basement doorway is of c1300 and the blocked original entrance doorway into the lord's hall lies above it. From the latter a straight stair in the east wall rises to the lord's bedroom and then up to the battlements, where there is a corbelled parapet, probably of c1300. Both the upper rooms are now refurnished in a fairly convincing medieval fashion.

South of the keep is the 14th century gatehouse with a gabled roof running north-south. The drawbridge was the only real deterrent to intruders. From here it is necessary to zig-zag (very unusual) through a range to reach the court. This range lying east of the gatehouse contains a pair of 7m long by 5m wide chambers. Originally they formed an undercroft with a hall above but in a late 15th century remodelling, when a stair in a south-projecting turret was made between the rooms, and they were given new windows the lower room became the hall, with a great chamber above it. The latter was refurnished again as a hall in the 1970s and has access through a room over the gateway to the rooms in the keep. The range continues east (although narrower and much remodelled) to contain a kitchen with a fireplace in the end wall. The range here replaces two facets of the polygonal 13th century curtain wall. The outer walls of the L-shaped block in the NW corner rise from the original curtain wall, which is pieced on the north by several windows and a doorway with a shell-hood. The north wing contains two fine living rooms with panelling and Victorian plaster ceilings. The dining room has Baroque pedimental doorcases and the old parlour a fine chimneypiece. The west wing contains bedrooms and a late 17th century scale-and-platt staircase. Excavations have revealed the lower parts of buildings of uncertain date and purpose on the eastern side of the courtyard.

RAGLAN CASTLE   SO 414083

In 1174 Raglan was held by Walter Bloet from Richard de Clare in return for the service of one Welsh knight at Usk Castle, and it is likely that the Bloets had a motte and bailey castle with timber buildings on this elevated (but not naturally defensible) site by c1100. Sir William ap Thomas married the heiress Elizabeth Bloet in 1406, and after her death in 1420 he remained here as a tenant of her son by an earlier marriage, Lord Berkeley, from whom he purchased the freehold in 1432. By then he had become the Steward of the lordship of Usk and Caerleon for Richard, Duke of York, and had married Gwladys, daughter of Sir David Gam, and widow of Sir Roger Vaughan (both were killed at the battle of Agincourt in 1415), which greatly increased his wealth. He is assumed to have begun replacing some of the older buildings on the site before his death in 1445. The south gate, at least must be his work, and probably also the hexagonal tower house known as the Yellow Tower of Gwent from the colour of its superb ashlar-facing.

However, it has been argued that the tower was actually built c1450 by his son Sir William Herbert. He was a strong supporter of the Duke of York against Henry VI, by whom he was outlawed in 1457. After the duke's son took the throne in 1461 as Edward IV, Sir William, whose forces had greatly contributed to Edward's victory over the Lancastrians at Mortimer's Cross became all-powerful in Wales, holding many offices and continuing to fight Lancastrian resistance. After his capture of Harlech in 1468 he was created Earl of Pembroke. It is fairly certain that he was responsible for a second building campaign accounting for the main gatehouse, the Kitchen Tower and most of the Fountain Court ranges which begun c1462 and continued until 1469, when Edward IV temporary lost power and the Earl of Pembroke and his brother Richard were captured and executed by the Earl of Warwick.

Interior of the Great Tower at Raglan

Gatehouse and Closet Tower at Raglan

There was then a long gap before any more work was resumed so what was achieved in these two campaigns together with whatever still remained of earlier buildings must have then been considered adequate. In 1478 William, 2nd Earl was obliged to exchange his title for that of Earl of Huntingdon as Edward IV required the earldom of Pembroke for his own eldest son. William was succeeded in 1491 by his daughter Elizabeth but his younger brother Walter remained in residence at Raglan and in 1502 entertained at Raglan Edward IV's daughter Elizabeth, Queen of Henry VII. Charles Somerset, husband of the heiress Elizabeth, became Baron Herbert of Raglan in 1504. Success as a courtier, statesman and soldier gained him a grant of the Earldom of Worcester from Henry VIII in 1514. His grandson William, 3rd Earl, who succeeded in 1548 and died in London in 1589, remodelled the central hall range, built another range NW west of it and also increased the size of the northern court by rebuilding the north range further out. This work seems to have been in progress c1586 and was completed by his son Edward, 4th Earl, who also added the White Gate further SE and the niches and statues of the walk around the moat of the Great Tower and the brick summer houses west of the bowling green to the south.

Charles I made the 5th Earl a marquis and his son Earl of Glamorgan as a reward for their support in the Civil War, when Raglan formed one of the chief Royalist strongholds and the estate reputedly contributed almost a million pounds to the royal cause. Security on the eastern side was improved by adding various outworks, including the now-destroyed Red Gate which is assumed to have been of brick. During the summer of 1646, when the King's cause was already lost, a garrison of 800 men was besieged by a force of 1500 men under Colonel Morgan. The attackers were later reinforced by more men fresh from the siege of Oxford, and by specialists such as Captain Hooper, who supervised the digging of siege-trenches during August whilst negotiations for surrender were in progress. The first Civil War came to an end when the Marquis finally yielded to Sir Thomas Fairfax on the 19th of August. A daily battering had destroyed the parapet on the Great Tower, damaged the gatehouse, destroyed a large window in the parlour, and breached the wall of the northern court near the Closet Tower. The castle was then plundered, the woods in the three parks were cut down, two of the six sides of the Great Tower destroyed and part of the southern curtain wall torn down.

The Great Tower at Raglan

Rear view of gatehouse

Parliament confiscated the Herbert estates but the grandson of the 1st Marquis of Worcester, Henry Somerset, later created Duke of Beaufort by Charles II, managed to regain some of them before the Restoration. In the 1660s, when he was regarded as the richest magnate in the kingdom, he built a new mansion at Badminton in Gloucestershire, which contains a fine carved overmantel of c1600 from the castle. The decay and plundering of the ruin for materials was stopped unusually early, after the fifth Duke succeeded in 1756. This was the age of the romantic revival and a few rooms in the gatehouse and Closet Tower were made habitable for visitors and the fallen parts of the Great Tower cleared away in 1821. The Duke of Beaufort is still the owner, although the ruin has been in State care (now Cadw) since 1938.

Raglan Castle has a hotchpotch of irregularly planned ranges with a number of polygonal towers set around two courtyards, between which is a range containing the great hall and chapel side by side. The Fountain Court to the south probably represents the bailey of the early castle and the Great Tower almost certainly stands on what remains of the motte. Ashlar-faced almost throughout and with machicolated parapets still remaining in a crumbled state on the main gatehouse and Closet Tower, the buildings are extremely impressive despite their very ruinous condition. They have an aura of military strength even though some of the defensive features were mostly for show. Some of the gunports would have been difficult to use in practice, as the Civil War defenders no doubt soon discovered.

Even though its fifth storey and machicolated parapet were destroyed in 1647, the Great Tower still commands the site. A hexagon 17m in diameter over walls 3.2m thick above a battered base (of rubble, contrasting with the fine ashlar above) it was once the finest medieval tower in South Wales. Four of its sides still rise through four storeys to a height of nearly 18m. The basement has both a fireplace and a well and was probably used both to store and prepare food, despite being lighted only by crossloops with oillets at all four extremities, set above circular gunports. The small square room walled off on the west side was probably a strongroom. The tower was entered at the level above, there being two bascule-type drawbridges suspended side-by-side from single beams. The drawbridge normally used was quite narrow and the second bridge was presumably only for ceremonial use. No parallel to this arrangement exists elsewhere in Britain, although it can be seen on a number of towers in France. Above this level were three large and splendid private chambers reached by a spiral stair beside the entrance. In each of these levels at least one of the windows was of two lights. Surrounding the tower, reached by a doorway cut through its base by the stair, is a low hexagonal chemise added in the 1460s with semi-circular corner turrets containing crossloops. One turret has a postern to the surrounding wet moat and another has a latrine. This wall rising straight out of the moat and making the lowest loops in the main tower redundant for defence, is overlooked by the rest of the castle, but it was possibly intended to be carried up higher with cannon mounted on platforms upon vaults over the turrets. The drawbridges were also then replaced by a stone bridge leading out over the moat from the parlour. Beyond the moat is a 17th century promenade with niches in the outer retaining walls in which were shell-work and figures of Roman emperors.

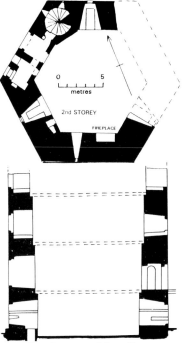

Plan & section of Great Tower

The hall block at Raglan

The mid 15th century great hall was 8.7m wide and 20.4m long. In the 1570s it was given a splendid new roof and a new north wall with plain four-light mullion and transom windows between a NW porch and a NE oriel lighting the dais end. The fireplace on this side has a flue which splits in two either side of a window above. The hammerbeam roof survived the destruction of the castle by several decades because of the difficulty of dismantling it. The ashlar-faced dais back wall has a panel with the arms of the 3rd Earl as a Knight of the Garter, which he received in 1570. A chapel, with its buttressed SW wall now entirely destroyed, was added in the 1460s against the hall south wall, in which earlier windows were blocked up, and in the 1570s a long gallery 38m long was extended over it and into a new polygonal bay added at the NW end. The bay had large and lofty windows with two transoms at this safe high level but lower down are thick walls with only small openings and a broadly splayed base in the medieval manner, so that despite its late date it preserved the defensibility of the enceinte. With it went a new range providing a spacious service area and two storeys of private rooms reached from the hall screens passage by a passage to a polygonal stair turret in the outer wall. In the upper room classical style details are used instead of the late medieval type of detailing used elsewhere in much of the mid to late 16th century work. The fireplace with paired figures in the adjoining long gallery and the scrolls supporting the seat in its spectacular NW end bay are also in the classical rather than late medieval style.

East of the hall was the parlour, with the drawing room above it, both originally with large, ornate windows overlooking the Great Tower moat. Another chamber extended down to the South Gate and had latrines in a turret adjoining it. There were further sumptuous apartments around the other two sides of the Fountain Court, named after a marble fountain in the form of a white horse which existed by 1587. Not much remains of the inner walls of these rooms and even the outer wall is missing between the South Gate and a latrine turret further west. A polygonal SW tower still standing high contained a grand staircase from the court to the upper rooms. After the more impressive new main gatehouse was added in the 1460s the South Gate (which had previously been the main entrance) served only to lead out to what became the bowling green platform. It has an off-centre passage leading space for a porter on the east, and was vaulted and had a portcullis.

South view of Raglan Castle

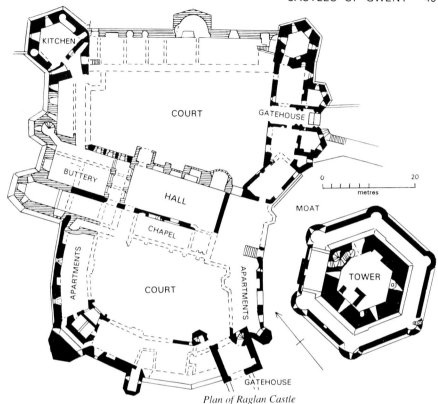

Plan of Raglan Castle

The Pitched Stone Court added in the 1460s provided service rooms and offices along the north and west sides. The large hexagonal NW tower contained a vaulted kitchen with a pair of fireplaces with ovens. Below was a vaulted wet larder with gunloops and above a suite of two rooms presumably for an important official. The Closet Tower at the NE corner contained a suite of rooms for the estate steward, and a topmost room probably for keeping the estate records. South of this tower lies the main gatehouse with thinly walled three storey polygonal towers flanking a passage closed by two portcullises, three pairs of doors and a drawbridge which was replaced by a stone bridge in the 16th century. The hexagonal form of the towers results in an angle rather than a flat face being presented to the field. The lowest rooms have gunports and the machicolated parapet was furnished with crossloops. Towards the court the gatehouse upper storey has a fine set of 15th century windows and then there is a 16th century top storey upon that. The service range between the Kitchen and Closet towers was rebuilt further north in the 16th century to widen the court, which was then re-cobbled. Only its outer wall, of defensible thickness despite the late date, and with reset gunloops in the projection halfway along, still stands.

The bowling green that gave Charles I so much pleasure during his visit in 1645 is probably part of an original Norman outwork later revetted in stone. The outwork extended further east and the White Gate was built in its ditch, resulting in subsidence to one of the thinly walled and poorly built towers. In front of it lay another court reached through the never competed Red Gate. Within the outer wall lay Castle Farm, built in the 1630s with "stables and barns...like unto a small town".

SKENFRITH CASTLE   SO 457203   F

Skenfrith was one of the Three Castles brought together as a single lordship along with Grosmont and White Castle by King Stephen in 1138. The three remained in common ownership until 1902. After the Welsh attacks on Abergavenny and Dingestow in 1182 the castles of Grosmont and Skenfrith were provisioned against a siege and in 1186-93 some £65 was spent on strengthening the earth and timber defences. Excavations had found traces of a stone internal building of that period. The existing castle, however, is mostly the product of a single building period begun probably in 1220 by Hubert de Burgh, who had been appointed Justiciar by King John, and created Earl of Essex by him in 1215. Hubert enjoyed great influence over the young Henry III, who was at Skenfrith in 1221 and 1222, but he lost the castle and several other possessions when he fell from grace in 1232. His rivals at court in turn fell from favour in 1234 and de Burgh eventually got the castles back, only to lose them again in 1239. Skenfrith was then placed in the custody of Waleran the German, who roofed the keep and built a new chapel in 1244. Henry III granted the Three Castles to Prince Edward in 1254 and then transferred them to his younger son Edmund in 1267. About that time the vulnerable south wall was strengthened by adding against the middle of it a solid D-shaped tower, a precaution necessitated by the growing strength of Llywelyn ap Gruffydd. There are no signs of later alterations and the castle, rarely used by the earls and then dukes of Lancaster, fell into decay. In the 20th century it was acquired by the National Trust and is now maintained on their behalf by Cadw.

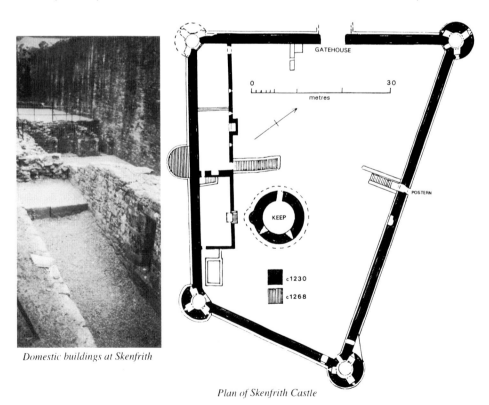

Domestic buildings at Skenfrith

Plan of Skenfrith Castle

Skenfrith Castle from the west

The castle has a single quadrangular court on a low-lying site beside the west bank of the River Monnow. The side facing the river (which has been diverted away from it) is 70m long and has a water-gate with a drawbar slot which was reached from the court by a flight of steps. This side lacks the quite high set batter on the outer face which the other shorter curtains have, whilst the internal offset was for supporting floors in a service range on this side. An each corner is a tower 7.5m in external diameter containing an unlit basement reached only by a trapdoor from above, and two upper levels with arrow loops which have all been torn out except for one high up in each of the towers by the river. All the curtains survive complete, although the gateway on the NW is now no more that a wide hole, and three of the towers are fairly complete, but the outer part of the western one is totally destroyed. There is a postern beside the SE tower and a doorway in the riverside curtain beside it led to a latrine. Excavations have shown that there was a 2m wide level berm around the walls, and then a stone-revetted moat 2.7m deep and 14m wide fed from the river. Also now revealed are the lower parts of a range containing a hall and solar on the SW side. The hall fireplace is original but the crosswall beyond it and the solar fireplace are later 13th century modifications. The range suffered from flooding and was then filled in and new apartments created at a higher level.

Close to the west range stands a circular tower keep 11.2m in diameter over walls 2.2m thick above a plinth battered to the first floor level, where there is a roll moulding. Wooden steps led up to a doorway into a reception hall, from which a spiral stair in a semi-circular turret led up to an upper room with two windows and a fireplace. The basement had its own doorway beneath the other one and communicated with the hall only via a trap-door in the floor. The basement loops are set above the roll-moulding and consequently the embrasures descend quite steeply into that room. Although the excavation evidence suggests that the keep was the last part of the castle to be built (apart from the modifications of c1270), its general appearance with round-headed openings suggests the contrary.

The Garrison Tower at Usk

TROSTREY CASTLE   SO 360043

The moated platform measuring 30m by 25m lying 180m south of the church towards the river is the site of a small stone-walled court built by the Marshals c1225 to replace an 11th century ringwork with a timber gatehouse and hall. The site was quarried for materials to build Trostrey Court (further east) in the 1580s. A house standing on the site in the Civil War period lasted until c1795.

The keep and gateway at Usk

USK CASTLE   SO 377010

After he was granted the lordship of Striguil (Chepstow) by Henry I in 1115 Walter Fitz-Richard established a secondary power centre based on a new castle and town at Usk. At his death in 1138 the Welsh seized Usk and held it until its recovered in 1174 by Gilbert de Clare (Strongbow). He is thought to have then strengthened the castle by building the keep. Usk passed to William Marshal in 1189 and, during his last years, from 1212 to 1219, he enclosed the bailey at Usk with stone walls flanked by round towers in response to the increasing threat of Llywelyn ab Iorwerth. One of his sons later remodelled the keep, and a document of 1289 records that Gilbert de Clare, Earl of Gloucester had recently built (i.e. rebuilt) the north tower to serve as a treasury, and had also formed another room on the top level of the Garrison Tower. After another Earl Gilbert was killed at Bannockburn in 1314 Usk passed to his sister Elizabeth de Burgh, for whom was built a new hall and chapel with a chamber block projecting northwards outside the curtain.

In 1368 Usk passed to Edmund Mortimer, Earl of March, and he or his son Roger, killed in 1398, walled in an outer bailey at a lower level on the east side. The castle withstood an attack by Owain Glyndwr in 1405, although the unfortified town below it was burnt. After Roger's son Edmund died in 1425 Usk passed to Richard, Duke of York, and merged with the Crown with the accession of Edward IV in 1461. Duke Richard left the lordship to be managed by Sir William ap Thomas of Raglan, and the latter's son Sir William Herbert in the 1460s remodelled the keep at Usk to serve him as an occasional residence in his capacity as steward. In the early 16th century the steward used the outer gatehouse and all the inner ward building were in decay. In 1556 a local man, Roger Williams, was accused of dismantling a barn and the main hall (probably just its roof and timber fittings) and taking the materials. A new house incorporating the outer gatehouse was later built to serve the stewards under the Dukes of Beaufort, and this still remains occupied by the present owners.

The solar block at Usk

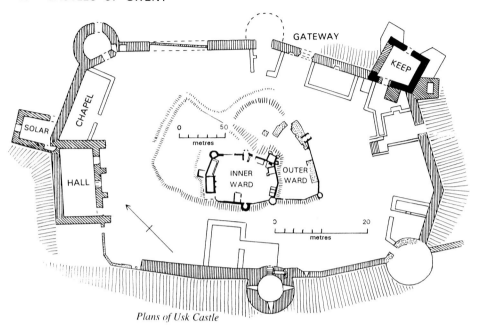

Plans of Usk Castle

The castle consists of an inner bailey about 75m by 44m lying at the south end of a wedge-shaped enclosure, the northern part of which must have contained gardens in the 14th century layout. To the east, at a lower level, is an outer bailey 90m long by 45m wide. The inner ward is roughly rectangular but with all the sides bowed out as if it were a crushed octagon. Although rebuilt or reduced in places William Marshal's 2m thick curtain wall of 1212-19 still surrounds the bailey except for a 12m wide gap on the NE and another west of the great hall. His Garrison Tower on the SW side stands almost complete, but only the base remains of another tower further south, whilst two other towers which must surely have existed by the 1220s on the NE side were either poorly built or were damaged during Richard Marshal's rebellion of 1233 or the troubles of the 1260s, and had to be replaced. Only buried footings remain of the small central 14th century tower on that side but the D-shaped north tower 10m in diameter dating from the 1280s is complete below the level of a lost corbelled-out top storey shown in a Buck brothers print of 1732. Crossloops remain on the east but the rest was refaced in the 15th century. Modern steps lead to an original upper doorway with rounded rebates like those at Caerphilly. The bailey gateway remained a simple arch closed by a portcullis in the curtain between the middle tower on this side and the keep at the east corner, a peculiar weakness.

The keep is a much altered building which would be 10m square but for the shorter length of the south wall. The vulnerable east wall is only 1.3m thick, and the other walls are 1.5m thick. The two blocked double-splayed round-headed openings in the south wall lighted a single upper room set over a basement. In the 13th century a latrine was provided in a projection where the curtain wall adjoins on the south and the walls reinforced by a massive plinth. In the mid 14th century the floor levels were changed and new opening made to create three storeys, and then in the 1460s the north wall was entirely rebuilt, without openings except for the upper fireplaces, and new windows and a basement doorway were opened in the east wall. A suite of other rooms was also then built within the angle of the curtain wall adjoining the keep.

The Garrison Tower has a solid base extending far below the court because of the fall of the ground on this side. It measures 10m in diameter and has four storeys linked by a spiral stair. The original round-headed entrance was at second storey level but a lower entrance was added during a remodelling in the 1280s when the third storey (which has access each side to the curtain wall-walk) was given a latrine, the top storey gained a fireplace, and a new corbelled parapet was added. NW of this tower the curtain has been thickened internally for a two storey suite of rooms.

At the NW end of the court are foundations of a chapel and a block which contained a hall 14.6m long by 7.2m wide on the upper level. The wall towards the court has buttresses and remains of window embrasures with seats, plus a fireplace for the undercroft. The hall has a west doorway towards a now-vanished set of service rooms. At the north corner a spiral stair gave access to a pair of upper private rooms with fireplaces in a block about 8m wide projecting outside the curtain. The attic over the hall was probably a later modification.

The northern part of the outer bailey has lost whatever defences it ever had, but there remain a gatehouse on the east, and curtain walls down to a round tower at the south corner, and from there back to join up with the inner ward, with a postern just beforehand. The round tower has a basement below the court and two upper storeys each with doorways from the court. Between it and the gateway a 16th or 17th century barn intrudes upon the wall-walk of the curtain, which is close to ground level since the curtain is mostly a retaining wall. Consequently there is a long flight of steps up to the court from the entrance passage of the gateway, in which is a portcullis groove. Above the gateway are windows with 19th century hoodmoulds and an oriel of that date cutting into the corbel table of the parapet.

The north (or Treasury) tower at Usk Castle

WHITE CASTLE SO 379168

Originally known as Llantilio, this fortress became known in the 13th century as White Castle from the white plaster coating of the external walls, fragments of which remain. The earthworks probably existed by 1137 when King Stephen confirmed the passing of Payn Fitz-John's lands (including Llantilio) via his daughter to her husband Roger, son of Milo of Gloucester. Henry had given Payn the lands of Hugh de Lacy, Lord of Ewyas, who had won quite a lot of territory from the Welsh before his death in 1115. Roger may have built the square tower keep at Llantilio. Henry II's Pipe Rolls record minor sums spend on maintaining and garrisoning the castle from 1155 onwards. The larger sum of £128 spent on the defences by the sheriff of Hereford in 1184-6 must refer to the building of the curtain wall. It is doubtful if that sum would have paid for the building of the keep as well.

King John granted the castle to Hubert de Burgh in 1201, but in 1205 transferred it to William de Braose, thus starting a dispute over ownership which was only settled in de Burgh's favour in 1219, although the de Braose family only resigned their claim in 1228. After Hubert fell from power in 1232 the castle was entrusted to Waleran the German, and he was still in charge in 1244, when a new hall, buttery and pantry were erected at the castle. The castle formed part of the lordship of the Three Castles granted by Henry III to Prince Edward in 1254. and transferred to his younger brother Edmund in 1267. During this period the lordship was threatened by the increasing power of Llywelyn ap Gruffydd and White Castle was considerably strengthened. The D-shaped outer ward must have been under construction in 1256-7, when work is recorded on an outer gateway with a portcullis and bridge. About the same time the inner ward was given a twin-towered gatehouse and four other towers. The internal buildings of the inner ward remained humble and there are no signs of any buildings in the outer ward, which suggests that the castle mainly served as an upland garrison and mustering-point for troops, which could camp in the outer ward, and that Grosmont served as the main seat of the lordship, despite being the smallest of the three castles. White Castle seems to have been maintained until the mid 15th century but was abandoned when seen by Leland in 1538. The ruins came into State guardianship in 1922 and are now maintained by Cadw.

White Castle

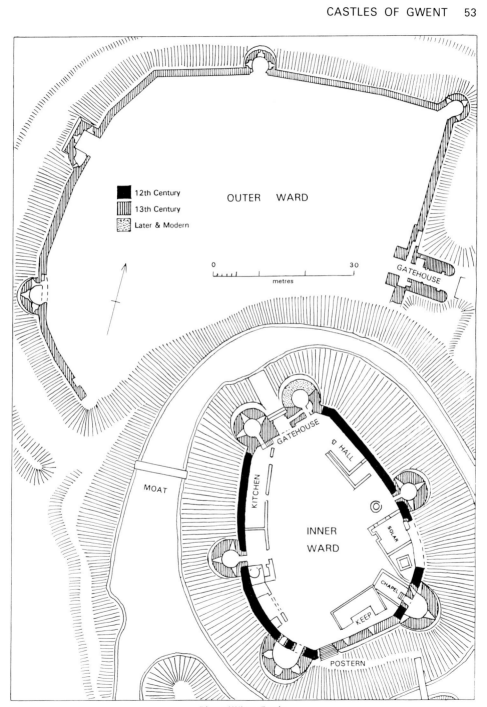

Plan of White Castle

The outer ward of White Castle

The egg-shaped inner bailey on top of the large motte is 45m long by 35m wide within a curtain wall 1.7m thick still complete up to the wall-walk except for a 9m wide gap on the east side. The towers set either side of the gateway passage and one on the east side of the court average 8m in diameter and each contained a circular room with three loops at courtyard level, a dark basement below, a storage room on the third storey and a fourth room at the level of the curtain wall-walk. The outer part of the eastern gateway tower has been rebuilt and now lacks any lower loops. The western tower is similar to the others but lacks a basement. The southern towers are large D-shaped structures 10m in diameter with for storeys. The ground level room of the SE tower formed the chancel of a chapel with a timber-framed nave in the courtyard. Between the two towers are foundations of the northern half of the 12th century tower keep which was about 10m square with walls 3m thick. Last repaired in 1257, it was demolished soon afterwards and the towers joined up by a new wall across the site of it. The new wall contains two loops and a postern leading out to a hornwork enclosed by a palisade lying beyond the wet moat of the motte. Along the eastern side of the court are the thin footings of a timber-framed hall and solar, with a well between them, whilst on the west side of the court were a timber-framed kitchen and offices.

The outer bailey measures 84m by 74m and has its own dry ditch. It is entered by a gatehouse on the west side with a passage 13m long, closed by a drawbridge and portcullis, and flanked by 2.5m thick walls with round outer ends, within one of which is squeezed a tiny room with a fireplace for a porter or guard. Stairs on the north side led to a now-destroyed latrine. The outer bailey has round towers about 6m in diameter at the NE corner, in the middle of the north side, and on the SW. There is also a two storey rectangular west tower 8.4m wide. There was a latrine where the west wall terminates above the inner moat.

BALLAN MOOR ST 488895 Low lying motte and bailey probably built c1086-1106 by the Ballon family, and later held by the Denfords.

CAER LICYN ST 390927 A farm track bisects a worn-down and very overgrown motte and bailey set on a commanding ridge.

DIXTON SO 518137 Excavation of the mound NE of the church revealed artifacts from the 11th and 12th centuries.

GOYTRE SO 354233 Motte on a spur high above the River Monnow.

HEN GWRT SO 395151 Held by the Bishops of Llandaff. Early 14th century square platform 36m square with wet moat surviving all round. An inner wall 1.2m thick surrounded a building 23m long by 18m wide. Rebuilt in 16th century but robbed of material in 1775 for building Llantilio Court. Free access.

LANGSTONE COURT ST 371895 Large bailey with motte upon which excavations revealed the base of a probably tower keep.

LLANGWM ST 427997 & SO 424011 Ringwork on ridge north of village. Traces of undefined earthwork around farmhouse on hill south of village.

LLANFAIR KILGEDDIN SO 349069 Motte on west bank of Usk east of village.

LLANVACHES ST 433920 Site of vanished stone castle north of village.

MOYNES COURT ST 427997 14th century gateway and oval moated enclosure to the south. Held in turn by de Knovils, Moigns, Hughes, Lysters, Lewis's.

MYNDDISLYWN ST 193938 Motte rising 5m from ditch to summit 14m across, to south of church on ridge elevated at nearly 300. See plan on page 4.

NEWCASTLE SO 447172 Tree-clad motte 6m high and bailey behind farmhouse.

PENRHOS SO 409132 Ditched motte 5m high with a moated bailey around it.

PEN-Y-CLAWDD SO 310200 Low, ditched motte behind farmhouse.

TRECASTLE SO 452070 17th century farmhouse within bailey platform with sections of wet moat. Oval motte 6m high on north side of platform.

TRELLECK SO 500054 Mound 5m high south of church. Mentioned in 1231. Destroyed by Welsh in 1295, then abandoned. Remains of town ramparts.

TREVEDDW SO 330217 Damaged tree-clad mound still partly 5m high. See p4.

TWYN-Y-GREGEN SO 363096 Mound beside stream close to the A40.

WOLVES NEWTON ST 449999 The farmhouse of Gwrt-y-Gaer stands on the site of the NE corner of an oval platform with ramparts and a wet ditch.

A few other earthwork sites are described along with the stone castles near them.

SELECTED LIST OF MOATED SITES IN GWENT

COED CWNWR ST 413994   GREAT CIL LLWCH SO 383138
LLANMARTIN ST 390895   PENCOED ST 404893

Motte at Trelleck

GAZETTEER OF CASTLES IN GLAMORGAN

ABERAVON CASTLE   SS 763902

A rectangular platform 54m long by 48m wide with a dry surrounding moat and a tiny central mound possibly covering the stump of a stone keep was removed to make way for terraced houses in 1895, and a 12m long masonry foundation was then revealed. Probably of Norman origin, the castle suffered destruction in 1153 by Maredudd and Rhys ap Gruffydd of Deheubarth on behalf of Morgan ap Caradog. They are supposed to have removed a great amount of plunder. The castle was rebuilt later and was still intact in 1485. Leland mentions only the "poore village" in 1538, but in the 1680s Edward Lloyd refers to a "ruinous castle".

BAGLAN CASTLE   SS 756923

The earthworks and buried footings of this castle lie in woodland east of the church. At the west end of a promontory lay a hall block or keep about 12m long by 9m wide, east of which was a small court about 10m wide. A stream has eroded the south end of the site. Probably of 13th century date, this castle, known as Plas Baglan, was later a cultural centre for bards and minstrels. Dafydd ap Gwilym is associated with it. The Lewis family acquired the estate in the 16th century but abandoned the cramped site in favour of Baglan Hall, now itself gone.

BEAUPRE CASTLE   ST 009721   F

The Bassets owned Beaupre from at least the late 14th century until they conveyed it to Christopher Brewster in 1709, the family fortunes having suffered through their being Royalists who were heavily fined by Parliament in the 1640s. The house has been known as Old Beaupre since a new house was built further north in the 19th century. The original hall block of c1300 may predate the Basset ownership. East of the hall is a gateway passage, now blocked, and beyond is an added range 6m wide, of tower-like form with a vaulted basement and corbelling high up, although there was only one full upper storey and a low attic in the roof, without any battlements. The private rooms lay west of the hall towards a slope to a stream. Another wing to the SE is still used as a farmhouse, and there are two more co-joined medieval blocks forming a second hall and chamber to the south, but there is no evidence that the medieval courtyard (not open to the public) was fully walled to make it defensible.

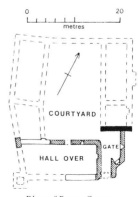

Plan of Barry Castle

Beaupre Castle from the west

Sir Rice Mansel occupied the house from 1516 to 1559 as husband of the heiress Elinor Basset. He remodelled the hall, blocking the medieval windows and replacing them with a huge new six-light window, and he also added a new four storey wing north of the private chambers. It has a scale-and-platt staircase in the middle leading to private upper rooms with latrines at the north end. This range later became the west side of a new northern court enclosed on the east by thin double walls connected by a vault over a void to support a wide wall-walk, and there is a four storey gatehouse block on the north. The gatehouse has an outer arch with a drawbar slot surmounted by an armorial panel with the date 1586, when Richard Basset inherited Beaupre, and the initials of him and his wife Catherine. The interior of the rectangular turret added to the court NW corner was reached only from the battlements and may have been a store for game, a cistern or even an ice-house. In 1600 Richard Basset added a remarkable new porch in front of the hall block. It has paired columns, Doric style at the bottom, then Ionic and finally Corinthian at the top. It has ashlar sides and was probably made in the Bath area.

The gatehouse of Barry Castle

BARRY CASTLE   ST 102673   F

Barry is named after the de Barri family, who held the manor here in the 11th century in return for service to the Umfravilles. No earthworks survive of an early castle and the existing building was begun probably by Lucas de Barry in the late 13th century. This branch of the de Barries died out in 1349 and the estate passed to the St Johns of Fonmon. The castle was ruinous when visited by Leland c1538. Later in the 16th century the south wall was demolished and a cottage, later used by William Wilkin as a tavern, was built into the shell. In the 18th century it was called Castle House. The ruins were cleared out and the site excavated in the 1970s.

The 13th century east and west ranges about 7 to 8m wide with a 12m wide courtyard between them, have gone except for the plain south wall of the east range. More survives of the south range added by John de Barry after the revolts of 1316 and 1321, when a curtain wall was built to link the parts. This new range had a hall 16m long by 6.4m wide above a basement. Adjoining at the east end is a gateway passage 2m wide which had a portcullis operated from a chapel above with a piscina and east and south window. There is a staircase to the lost battlements at the SE corner of the hall, and there was a latrine turret clasping the SW corner.

The leaning SE tower at Caerphilly

Tower on the north dam at Caerphilly

CAERPHILLY CASTLE   ST 156871   C

In 1267 Gilbert de Clare seized Senghennydd from Gruffydd ap Rhys, who was imprisoned at Cardiff. Earl Gilbert had been authorised by Henry III to take over the lands of Welsh lords who supported Llywelyn ap Gruffydd. Work began in April 1268 on a huge new castle to consolidate de Clare's power in the area. Inspired by the recent siege of Kenilworth, where a rebel garrison held the whole military might of England at bay for several months from within a large castle protected by an artificial lake held in by a fortified dam, the new castle had a quadrangular court with an outer wall rising from the waters of such a lake held in by blocking the valley with a defensible dam. Llywelyn occupied the upland northern part of Senghennydd during the summer of 1268 and burnt the wooden parts of the incomplete castle in October 1270. By the autumn of 1271, when a truce was made, and the castle was handed over to the bishops of Lichfield and Worcester as arbitrators over the disputed lands, the main platform with its two lines of defence and the hornwork on the west and the southern part of the dam on the east must have been almost complete.

Llywelyn refused to give homage to Edward I when the latter returned from a crusade in 1274. He was defeated in a campaign in North Wales in 1277, by which time Earl Gilbert had started a second campaign at Caerphilly, heightening the west and south walls of the inner ward, and adding the kitchen tower to the latter. A third campaign probably in progress when Llywelyn was killed in 1282, saw the extension northwards on the dam to create the north lake. In a fourth phase probably shortly before the earl died in 1295 the east wall of the northern dam was heightened and then three towers built against it.

Caerphilly Castle

After the de Clare estates passed to three sisters in 1314 Edward II appointed firstly Bartholomew de Badlesmere and then Payn Turberville as keepers of Glamorgan. Their poor treatment of the local Welsh goaded the latter into a rebellion in 1316 led by Llywelyn Bren, who had been de Clare's former agent. Llywelyn attacked Caerphilly with a large force and although he was unable to make any more impact on the castle than to burn the south gateway of the dam, the town was devastated and those attending a court outside the castle gate were killed or captured. Edward II then handed over Glamorgan to the even more unpopular Hugh le Despenser the younger, who was married to the eldest of the de Clare heiresses. Hugh remodelled the hall at Caerphilly and added a large new kitchen on the south side. When Edward II's estranged consort Queen Isabella and her lover Roger Mortimer invaded England in 1326 the king took refuge with Hugh at Caerphilly. Hugh was summarily hanged after he and Edward were captured by the Marcher lords near Llantrisant. Sir Edward de Felton held the well-provisioned castle, which contained much of Edward II's belongings and treasure, against the queen's forces led by William la Zouche until March 1327, when the pardon offered to the garrison of 130 men was extended to include the Despenser heir. The latter only obtained Caerphilly when his mother died in 1337. This woman had custody of the Glamorgan lordship from 1328 but was abducted by William la Zouche, who forcibly married her and besieged the castle again until it was relieved by Roger Mortimer.

The later Despencers, and the Beauchamps who succeeded them in 1415 had many other residences elsewhere. An outer gatehouse used as a prison was repaired c1430 but the rest was left to decay and was ruinous when John Leland visited it in 1538. Courts were still being held in a gatehouse in the 1550s but in 1583 the Earl of Pembroke, then owner, allowed Thomas Lewis to removed cut stones from the ruin for reuse in his nearby house, The Van. The lakes were drained, caused some subsidence of the islands as they dried out. Parliament had a redoubt built to command the castle from the NW in 1647, and although there is no record of any Royalist attempt fortify the ruin or of its destruction, the loss of the outer parts of all the inner ward corner towers and the east gatehouse towers looks like the effect of slighting. The 3rd Marquis of Bute had the hall re-roofed c1870, and the 4th Marquis had several of the fallen parts rebuilt in 1928-39 and the site generally tidied up. The lakes were refilled after the castle had passed into state care in 1950. It is now in the care of Cadw.

Caerphilly Castle has a quadrangular inner ward 75m long by 44m wide enclosed by a wall 2.4m thick and 4.5m high to the wall-walk. At each corner is a drum tower 11m in diameter and 20m high containing a basement lighted by loops and two lofty and comfortable upper rooms with trefoil-headed lancet windows and fireplaces which are reached by spiral stairs set beside the entrance passages. Only tumbled fragments remain of the NE tower, whilst the outer part of the SE tower, one of the few parts to retain original crenellations, leans dramatically outwards probably as a result of being undermined and blown up in 1647-8. It retains a top storey fireplace and holes for the beams of hoarding below the parapet. The outer parts of the western corner towers were rebuilt in the 1930s. There are twin-towered gatehouses to the east and west, two posterns in the north wall (which is now partly surmounted by modern hoarding) and a south postern closed by two portcullises with steps down to the lake. The east gatehouse is similar in layout to another at the de Clare castle of Tonbridge in Kent, and there are foundations of a third at their castle of Llangynwyd. It was designed as a self-contained citadel with private chambers and a hall for the use of the constable on the second and third storeys respectively. The side walls of the towers are thickened partly to allow space for latrines and other small rooms including an oratory at hall level. They rise above the main battlements to shield steps to the tops of the round stair turrets set on the inner corners. The round outer faces of the towers were entirely rebuilt in 1931-3 but the inner part is original work except for the parapet. The gateway passage was closed by two sets of doors with portcullises in front of them and the guardroom doorways opened off the passage between these two barriers. There were machicolations in the passage roof and the inner arch is commanded by a slot in the wall above. The smaller west gatehouse has stairs in thickness of the inner corners rather than in projecting turrets. The vaulted lower rooms have doorways with drawbar slots entered directly from the court. Above was just a single hall with a central fireplace and two rather damaged east windows. On this gatehouse little beyond the battlements has been restored.

Surrounding the inner ward at a distance of about 15m is a retaining wall rising high above the lake, but with only a parapet (mostly rebuilt) above the level of the middle ward thus enclosed. This ward has twin-towered gatehouses set in front of those of the inner ward and a postern on the north side. The outer parts of the gatehouses were built first and the rectangular inner parts added later. The west gatehouse remained in use as a courtroom and has 16th century upper fireplaces. The middle ward contained a store on the west, a cistern (much restored) on the east and the service buildings adjoining the south side of the great hall in the inner ward.

Caerphilly before restoration started

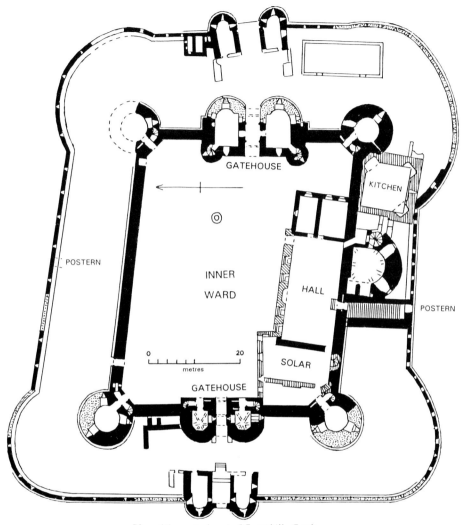

Plan of the central part of Caerphilly Castle

The hall 22m long by 11m wide on the south side of the inner ward is roofed in six bays corresponding to the divisions of the north wall of the 1320s with a NE doorway, a central fireplace and four huge ogival-headed window embrasures with ball-flower ornamentation. At that time the kitchen with a vaulted brewhouse below it within a now very ruinous D-shaped tower projecting from the south wall (not shown to the public) was suplimented by another kitchen with corner fireplaces in a now very ruined block squeezed in beside the SE tower. The suite of north-facing private rooms west of the hall probably saw little use after Despencer's death in 1326. They were once served by a latrine block outside the curtain. Over the pantry and buttery east of the hall are a solar once reached by external steps and a chapel south of it with a large east window (none of those rooms are open to the public).

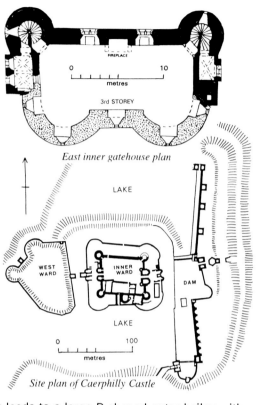

East inner gatehouse plan

The western gatehouse at Caerphilly

Site plan of Caerphilly Castle

The middle ward western gateway leads to a large D-shaped outer bailey with just a low retaining wall flanked by two round bastions on the vulnerable NW side. Between them was a an outer gate with a drawbridge from the flat ground beyond, north of which is a Civil War period redoubt on the site of a Roman fort. This outer ward was known in Welsh as "Y Weringaer" (People's fort) so it was evidently a refuge for the townsfolk. A bank extends round from this work to join up with the dam on the east, and this divided the main south lake of 1268-71 with the slightly later north lake. The dam has a wide central platform with a round SE bastion and then, beyond the base of a water mill, there is a narrower round-ended south platform with a heavily buttressed east wall ending with a square tower which controlled the lake level sluices. There is a D-shaped tower facing south and a twin-towered gatehouse facing west. The gatehouse was mostly rebuilt in the 1930s, especially the northern tower, although the spurred tower bases are original. As first built the gatehouse towers were open-backed and the chambers over were created later.

In the 1280s a narrow extra dam platform was extended northwards to a twin-towered outer gate. A third, eastward-facing two storey twin-tower gatehouse was then inserted into the NE corner of the central platform. The towers of both these new gatehouses have semi-octagonal outer faces rising from square bases with triangular spurs, as do the series of three towers later added against the north dam east wall to help buttress it. These towers have now cracked away as a result of land settlement caused by drying out when the lakes were drained. The east side of the whole length of the dam was protected by an outer moat with a bank beyond it.

Hall fireplace at Candleston

The tower house at Candleston

CANDLESTON CASTLE   SS 872773   F

The name Candleston is derived from the Cantilupes, who built a fortified manor house here in the 14th century. A two storey domestic range closed off the straight landward side of a D-shaped court 33m by 26m. Added slightly later against the hall at the SE end is a tower measuring 7.9m by 6.4m containing a solar over a dark cellar with a very flat vault. The solar has a latrine in one corner and a fireplace with its back wall knocked out. It was reached from below by a straight stair in the extra thick SW wall. A blocked doorway off the stairhead opened onto the wall-walk 2m above the court (but higher above the exterior) of a now very fragmentary curtain wall 1.1m thick. The hall was rebuilt c1500 and has a fine fireplace of that period backing onto the tower. The estate lost its value because of encroachment by sands but the 17th century wing projecting into the court shows the house remained occupied, although the northern half of the main block was ruinous when the building was patched up as a temporary residence for Sir John Nichol until his new house at Merthyr Mawr was completed in 1808. The eastern stables are of that period. The building is now a ruin.

Plans of Candleston Castle

CARDIFF CASTLE   ST 180767   O

There are good reasons for assuming that this castle was founded by William I on his way back from an expedition to St Davids in 1081. It became the caput of the lordship of Glamorgan won from the Welsh by Robert Fitz-Hamon in 1093. He died of wounds received in battle in 1107 and his daughter Mabel brought the lordship to Henry I's illegitimate son Robert, created Earl of Gloucester c1120. Earl Robert probably built the stone shell keep, either before 1126, when Henry I's elder brother Duke Robert of Normandy (captured back in 1106) was kept a prisoner at the castle until he died in 1134, or in the period of tension after King Henry's death in 1135, when the Welsh were threatening to revolt. In 1158 Ifor Bach, Lord of Senghenydd scaled the bailey walls in a surprise night attack and abducted the then earl, William, and his wife and son. They were kept prisoner in a wooded fastness until the lands taken from him by the Normans had been restored. The town was burnt in a Welsh attack shortly after William's death in 1183.

The lordship of Glamorgan passed to Henry II's youngest son John upon his marriage to Isabel, the heiress in 1189. John divorced her in 1199 but retained the lordship throughout his reign. After her death in 1217 the lordship passed to Isabel's nephew Gilbert de Clare. The castle was captured by Richard Marshal during his rebellion of 1233. It was Gilberts namesake grandson who pushed back the frontiers of his Welsh estates in the late 1260s and built new castles at Caerphilly and Morlais, as well as the eastern wall of the inner bailey at Cardiff. After his son Gilbert III was killed at Bannockburn in 1314 the lordship eventually passed to his sister Elizabeth, married to Edward II's unpopular favourite Hugh le Despenser. In 1321 the antagonised local barons assembled a force of 11,000 men and stormed all of Hugh's castles in the lordship, including Cardiff. Despencer recovered his position after the royalist victory at Boroughbridge early in 1322 but he was captured and executed at Hereford in 1326. Hugh's great nephew Thomas, who became Lord of Glamorgan in 1394, obtained the Earldom of Gloucester in 1397, but was executed in Bristol in 1400 for rebelling against Henry IV. His widow Constance regained the estates in 1401 by which time the castle was under threat from Owain Glyndwr's rebellion. Owain eventually captured and sacked both the town and castle in 1404. Accounts of that period referring to munitions and garrison payments mention guns and powder and balls for them.

The motte and shell keep at Cardiff

The domestic range at Cardiff

    Thomas and Constance left a daughter Isabel who married firstly Richard Beauchamp, Earl of Worcester, and then in 1423 as her second husband, another Richard Beauchamp, Earl of Warwick. A leading statesman, with custody of the young Henry VI, he built a new suite of apartments on the west side of the inner bailey. His son was created a Duke in 1444 but died the following year. Richard Neville, son of the Earl of Salisbury, married Richard's sister Anne and thus obtained the Lordship of Glamorgan. He was created Earl of Warwick in 1450 and was the famous Warwick the Kingmaker who helped put Edward IV on the throne in 1461. He was killed at the battle of Tewkesbury in 1471. The heiresses were both married to Edward IV's brothers and in 1474 Richard, Duke of Gloucester became Lord of Glamorgan, which he held until his defeat and death as king at Bosworth in 1485. The castle was then held until his death in 1495 by Henry VII's uncle Jasper Tudor, Duke of Bedford. The lordship was later held by the Somersets, Earls of Worcester. None of these lords since the 1440s made much use of the castle and Leland described parts of it as being in ruins.

The crosswall and Black Tower at Cardiff

In 1551 Edward VI granted the lordship of Glamorgan to William Herbert, whom he created Earl of Pembroke and Lord Herbert of Cardiff. In 1555 Rawlins White was held prisoner in the Black Tower before being burnt at the stake for heresy. In the 1570s Henry, 2nd Earl of Pembroke renovated the apartments at Cardiff. The 4th Earl of Pembroke supported Parliament in 1641 but the castle was soon captured by the Royalists and held until Sir Richard Bassett was forced to surrender it to a Parliamentary force in September 1645. Local Royalists besieged the castle in February 1646 but were dispersed by a relief force led by Major General Laugharne. Another Royalist force was beaten off in 1648. The castle was described in 1666 as "partly demolished and out of repair" although a number of rooms were still in use in 1673. In 1704 the castle passed to the Windsors and in 1766 an heiress brought it to John Mountstuart, who succeeded as 4th Earl of Bute in 1792, and was made Marquis of Bute in 1796. He began renovations to the apartments and landscaping, although the work was left unfinished when his son died in 1794. A more major scheme of work, creating the Victorian fantasy that Cardiff is today, was executed in the 1870s by William Burges for the 3th Marquis. Reconstruction of the Roman walls began in the 1890s and continued under the 4th Marquis until the 1920s. The 5th Marquis handed over the castle to the city as a public amenity in 1947.

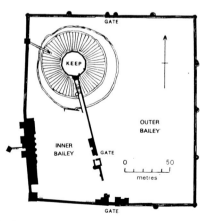

Plans of Cardiff Castle

The domestic range at Cardiff

William I's great 10m high motte lies in the NW corner of a Roman fort 200m by 180m the walls of which date from c280, although there were earlier and small forts on the site. The Normans divided off the western third as an inner bailey with stone walls upon what was left of the Roman ones, whilst the remainder became a large outer bailey with an earth rampart raised over the remains of the Roman wall. Between 1889 and 1923 the earth bank was removed to reveal the 3m thick Roman wall still partly standing 5m high, and they were then built up to a height of about 10m, higher than the ever were in Roman times. On the south side the Roman remains are preserved on view in a gallery. Originally there were eighteen polygonal bastions set at the corners, in pairs flanking the north and south gates, and at intervals along the sides. They were solid apart from where guard chambers were needed by the gateways and for a postern in the eastern central bastion. Eleven of these bastions have been rebuilt as part of the modern restoration.

The 12th century polygonal shell wall 1.7m thick enclosing a court 24m across on the motte is unusually well preserved. There is a fireplace recess on the west side. Of a hall block 9.6m wide which was laid across the interior c1300 only the SE gable end remains projecting slightly from the shell wall. Beside it, facing south, is a polygonal fronted gatehouse of the same period, the floors and roof of which were reinstated in the 1880s. Luckily a plan to cover the court with a dome was not proceeded with. The hall gable and gatehouse each have one 16th century upper window. A long set of steps with walls on both sides and a polygonal 15th century well turret on the west side continue the line of the inner bailey east wall and climb up the site of the motte to the keep. Both this barbican and the 11th century bailey east wall 1.8m thick and 6m high, plus a 13th century tower beside the gateway, were reduced to their footings as part of the landscaping efforts of Capability Brown in the 1770, a major act of vandalism. He also had the moat around the motte filled in but luckily this was reinstated in the 1880s. The south end of the barbican formed a tower and had a portcullis and a door secured with a drawbar.

In the acute angle between where the crosswall between the baileys met the Roman outer wall is the 13th century Black Tower, which is 8.6m square and 18m high to the top of its restored battlements. It contains a vaulted basement and three upper rooms (now a museum) reached by an external stair over the stump of the bailey crosswall and then a spiral stair in a polygonal 15th century NE turret. On the west is a an added 15th century wing containing smaller rooms with latrines. From the lowest one there is access to the restored wall-walk of the inner bailey south wall which is 11th century work 2.4m thick upon a thicker Roman base. At the SW corner is the 40m high Clock Tower, an entirely new structure of 1869-73. Excavations in the 1970s have revealed the foundations of the long buttresses late 14th century Shire Hall which lay in the outer bailey not far east of the inner bailey wall.

The apartments back onto the 3m thick west wall, which is partly 11th century but with Roman work standing high in places, and with 19th century windows and passages cut through, especially on the upper two of the three levels, which are now called the Library and the Banqueting Hall. In the middle is a 15th century block with a vaulted basement and what are assumed to have originally formed lower and upper halls with private chambers at the north ends. Four polygonal turrets face east, three containing ornate bay windows, but the SE turret contains a spiral stair connecting all three levels. Other windows between the turrets have been restored. Built against the outer wall at this point is the Beauchamp Tower, also early 15th century. An octagon 7m across rising with spurs from a square base to a restored machicolated parapet rising 21m above the ground outside, it now contains a wide late 19th century staircase and has a spire within the parapet. The Herbert Tower 6m square further south is a late 16th century structure, whilst the Bute Tower 7m wide further north is late 18th century, as is the northern part of the range containing the dining room which adjoins it. The southern part of the range, with two more polygonal east turrets, and ending in the seven storey Guest Tower, are late 19th century. The late 19th century features and fittings designed by William Burges in all the rooms, although of very great interest, lie outside the scope of this book.

The town had earth and timber defences by 1185, and had stone walls on the east and south sides by the end of the 13th century. The castle lay on the north and the marshes of the Taff protected the west side. The North Gate lay close to the SE corner of the castle, the East or Cokkerton Gate lay at the junction of Friary and Queen streets, the South Gate closed off St Mary's Street, and the West Gate lay be the SW corner of the castle. The gates are shown on John Speed's map of 1610 and were demolished between 1781 and 1802. A reconstruction of the West Gate was erected beside the castle in the 1930s.

CASTELL COCH   SO 132826   C

This sandstone building (hence the name meaning Red Castle) is chiefly known as a spectacular romantic folly with remarkable interior decorations built in the 1870s by William Burges for the 3rd Marquis of Bute. However, it is built upon the lower parts of a genuine 13th century castle, thought to be part of the barrier of castles founded by Gilbert de Clare to protect his lordship of Glamorgan against the Welsh. As begun probably in the 1260s it had a circular SW tower keep 12m in diameter above a square base with pyramidal spurs, and an adjoining hall over a basement set on the south side of a tiny D-shaped court. It stands on a platform commanding the gorge of the Taff and was protected from higher ground to the north by a deep dry moat, from the bottom of which the walls rose with a very broadly battered base to encase the slope of was probably originally a 12th century motte. The keep contained a vaulted room 5.4m in diameter at the level of the court, another below it, a larger room above and possibly a fourth storey with a conical roof like it has now.

Castell Coch

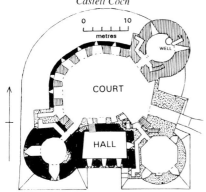

Plan of Castell Coch

Castell Coch

The two eastern circular towers and the square gatehouse between them, were superior ashlar-faced buildings added probably in the 1270s. These parts were more ruinous than the remains of the first campaign of building and not much remained of the towers above their vaulted basements below courtyard level. This was especially true of the SE tower (which has an octagonal basement), now confusingly labelled the keep, and rebuilt with thinner upper walls to contain a suite of rooms with fantastic details. The NE tower contains a well. The curtain wall was thickened during the second building phase to provide a series of embrasures at courtyard level and a wall-walk (now roofed over), giving two fighting galleries.

CASTELL TALYFAN   ST 021772

There are slight traces here of a probable circular keep 15m in diameter, perhaps an addition by Richard de Clare. The castle reverted to him in 1246 on the downfall of Richard Siward, the presumed builder of the surrounding curtain wall 1.5m thick enclosing a court 48m by 38m. Most of the ruins were dismantled for materials between 1828 and the 1860s, leaving only footings of the curtain plus a 4.5m high fragment incorporated in a farmhouse of c1700 (now also ruined) and part of a latrine turret later added to the keep. The castle was repaired by the Despencers after being wrecked by their enemies in 1321 and remained in use until the 15th century.

CASTLETON, ST ATHAN   ST 024684

The eastern block of a farmhouse lying above a steep gorge east of the village has thick walls probably remaining from a castle of the Nerber family. It was rebuilt in the 1520s by Howell Adam, passed to Sir John Popham, and was later sold to the Stradlings. A medieval gatehouse north of the house has been converted into a barn.

COITY CASTLE   SS 923816   F

Although there is no mention of the castle itself until King John's reign, historical circumstances make it likely that Payn Turberville had a castle here c1100 as part of his overlord Robert Fitz-Hamon's strategy for the subjugation of this district. Either his younger son Gilbert or the latter's son Payn II refortified the ringwork with a stone wall and tower keep in the late 12th century. It was Payn III who had temporary custody of the lordship of Glamorgan after Gilbert de Clare was killed in 1314, and whose repressive measures led to the rebellion of Llywelyn Bren in 1316. The castle was extensively rebuilt during the 14th century either by Payn's son Gilbert IV or his brother Richard who succeeded to Coity in the 1350s.

By the 1380s the castle had passed to Sir Lawrence Berkerolles, husband of Richard's sister Catherine Turberville. In 1404 Prince Henry mustered an army at Hereford to relieve Sir Lawrence, then under close siege at Coity by Owain Glyndwr's forces. Henry IV himself made another attempt to relieve the castle in September 1405 but the weather turned against him and the rebels plundered his baggage train. There is evidence that the Welsh breached the north walls of both the inner and outer wards of the castle, so presumably they managed to capture it, although this is unrecorded. When Sir Lawrence died in 1411 the castle was occupied by Joan, widow of Richard Vernon, a descendant of Margaret Turberville. This was challenged by William Gamage, grandson of Margaret's sister Sarah, who was besieging John in the castle in 1412, and who eventually won his case in court. The Gamages then lived at Coity and built the barn in the outer ward and the NE gatehouse of the inner ward. Both Leland in the 1530s and Merrick a few years later found the buildings generally in good repair. Robert Sydney acquired Coity on his marriage with Barbara, daughter of John Gamage in 1584. They lived elsewhere but members of the family continued to use the castle until the 18th century, but it was ruined by 1833, when it passed from the Wyndhams to the Earl of Dunraven. Some clearance took place in the 1860s and 70s and the castle was placed in state guardianship in 1929.

Inner ward from the west, Coity

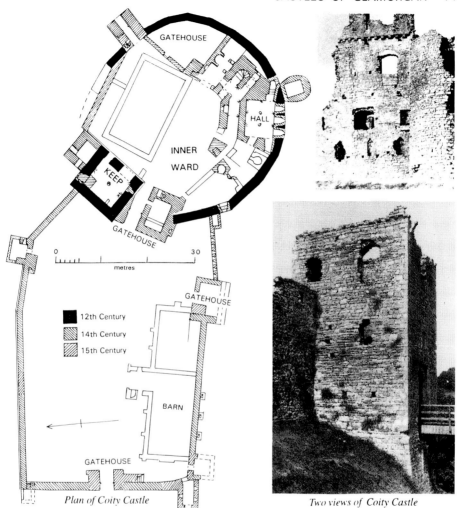

Plan of Coity Castle

Two views of Coity Castle

A late 12th century curtain wall 1.8m thick and 5m high encloses the circular inner ward about 40m across. On the west side is a contemporary tower keep measuring about 12m by 10m over walls 1.9m thick. In the 14th century the two lowest levels were given massive rib-vaults with central piers and a wing also with two levels of vaults, and latrines at second and third storey levels, was added at the north end. The building was again remodelled c1500 with new windows and fireplaces and both the main block and the wing were given a fourth storey, giving a total height to the top of the parapet of about 18m. Only the northern half of the west wall and most of the wing still stand above the level of the lowest vault. The two upper main rooms were reached by a stair inserted in the SW corner from which there was probably also access onto the battlements of the gatehouse immediately to the south. The gatehouse upper room (now destroyed) was reached directly from the court by a stair in its back wall. The gateway passage was closed by a portcullis and flanked on the south by a guard room.

South side of the outer ward at Coity

East of the wing the polygonal curtain wall was breached during the siege of 1404-5 and was later replaced by a straight length of wall running over a new NE gatehouse then added. This gatehouse measures 7m by 6.3m and contains two upper rooms reached by a spiral stair over a passage with a portcullis groove and a drawbar slot behind a door rebate. Towards the field both upper rooms had two-light windows, and two one has a second such window and a latrine in its SE wall. The lower room window remains complete and has a machicolation slot in its sill. The vaults of this room and the passage have fallen. The parapet was corbelled on the three outer sides but there were no machicolations. Between the keep and this gatehouse are footings 1m thick of the walls of a large medieval building of uncertain purpose, possibly an early hall, although if so it must have been aisled.

On the south side of the court lay a small (9m by 7m) hall with a solar above it. Below is a cellar rib-vaulted in three by two bays with a pair of octagonal piers. It has three lancets pierced through the curtain, and access to a postern. Between this cellar and the court is a rib-vaulted passage connecting with the various service rooms extending towards the gatehouse and with a wide spiral stair up to a lobby between the hall and the court. Projecting from the curtain at the hall SE corner is an ovoid tower providing three upper levels of latrines above a straight-sided cess pit, there being corbelling to carry the rounded faces higher up. This work is all 14th century, although the wing added to the NE to contain an upper chapel is 15th century, and the curtain wall parapet above the service rooms is also of that date. There is a hole in the curtain wall for the chapel east window. The arrangement of the basement passages around the main stair suggests that it was originally intended to breach the curtain behind the stair for the addition of a projecting chapel tower. The three windows in the outer wall at hall level, and the fireplace and two windows for the chamber above are insertions of c1500. The crosswall containing fireplaces and ovens in the service area is also of c1500. Above here were two 14th century private chambers, the western of which was in the 15th century provided with a latrine in a turret where the outer ward curtain adjoined. The segment of the court between the chapel block and the NE gatehouse was screened off by a wall 5m high, probably to create a working area for the wall seems too high for a garden.

The keep at Coity Castle

An outer ward 35m wide extends for 50m from the inner ward gateway to its own very ruinous 15th century west gatehouse. Although the ditch and counterscarp bank of the inner ward are well preserved the earthworks protecting the outer ward have been levelled. Except for the filling in of a breach made in the siege of 1405 the wall on the north side is all 14th century, with one small projecting tower, the outer part of which is destroyed. External steps led to a single upper storey. The west wall is also 14th century and has a blocked doorway with a drawbar slot at the NW, where there was probably a turret or tower. A 15th century turret projects westwards at the SW corner and adjoins the stump of a small tower projecting south which it seems to have replaced. Much of the south side is taken up with the footings of a large 15th century barn with buttressed walls and a north porch. Buttresses were added to the thin original 14th century outer wall here. East of the barn are footings of the strongly battered base of the south gate with a 16th century stone bridge over the moat in front of it. The gateway passage was flanked on the east side by a guard room and there was probably just one room above, as shown on a Buck brothers print of 1740, when this building was still roofed. The section of wall between here and the inner ward is 15th century work and has a series of embrasures with crossloops at ground level. The wall was heightened later.

South Gate of Cowbridge town defences

Ewenny Priory: site plan

COWBRIDGE TOWN WALLS SS 994746 V

Richard de Clare granted the town of Cowbridge a charter in 1254. It prospered and by c1300 had walls enclosing 30 acres. The South Gate measuring 6.8m by 6m with a passageway 3.2m wide was repaired in 1805, 1853, although its upper levels have gone. A length of the wall survives west of it. At the Butts it turned north to where the main road was straddled by the West Gate, demolished in 1754. It continued north to the end of Eagle Lane and then followed North Road. Beyond the North Gate, which was a mere postern leading out to meadows, a portion still remains. Behind the present Town Hall the wall turned south to East Gate, demolished in 1775, and then went SW to a bastion at the bottom of the school grounds.

DINAS POWIS CASTLE ST 147723 & 153717 F

The original seat of the de Somery family here was the partial ringwork with a court 50m by 35m defended on its weakest south side by multiple rampart and ditch system. Excavations in the 1950s found no evidence of previous use of the site in the Iron Age as previously claimed, although it was used during the Dark Ages. The court 67m long by 33m wide surrounded by a wall 1.7m thick still 6m high to the wall-walk on the NE and SE sides is thought to be of c1190-1200. Its NW end partly overlies the base of an abandoned earlier tower keep 18.3m by 13.4m over walls 3m thick. The curtain has embrasures at ground level on either side of the east corner and a SE gateway with a drawbar slot, a narrow NE postern, and a doorway on the base of the old keep. The postern was pointed-headed but the gateway is said to have been round-arched. After 1194 Dudley Castle in Staffordshire became the centre of the de Somery estates and there are no signs of later medieval work at Dinas Powys, although coins up to the 15th century were found on the site. In 1222 Henry III ordered the castle to be handed over to Gilbert de Clare, who had already made one attempt to take it from the Earl of Pembroke by force. It was later returned to the de Somerys, the last of whom, John, died in 1321. The castle then passed to the Suttons and was sold by them to Sir Matthew Cradock in the early 16th century. It was "al in ruine" when seen by Leland in 1536.

Ewenny: North Gate

0   3
metres

Cowbridge: South Gate

East corner of Dinas Powis Castle

EWENNY PRIORY   SS 913778   V

The early 14th century defences around the Benedictine priory must have been largely for show since there is no sign of a ditch, the east side facing higher ground is weak, and the wall enclosed an area 185m long by 125m wide which would have required a huge force to defend it. East of the north tower the wall made a re-entrant angle to adjoin the transept of the church. The north tower contains a ruinous living room with a later fireplace above a flat barrel-vaulted basement. A barn has replaced the wall between it and the north gate, which has a passage with a portcullis groove between thick side walls which have polygonal ends rising from spurred bases towards the field. The design recalls the Llanblethian gatehouse. Some 12th century work survives further in. The room above reached by a spiral stair was later converted into a dovecote. The wall then runs fairly complete out to the open-gorged circular NW tower with crossloops at two levels, and from there down the west side and back as far east as the south gate. Corbelling inside provides enough width at the top for a wall-walk. The south gate has a two bay 12th century passageway flanked on the east side by a semi-octagonal tower. The building was converted in to a summerhouse in the 19th century. From here the south wall is missing as far as the rectangular SE tower with a dovecote inserted in its upper storey. Only the lower part of the east curtain wall remains, with a postern halfway along it. See page 76.

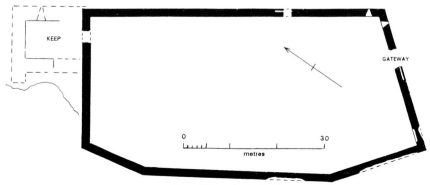

KEEP

GATEWAY

0   30
metres

Plan of Dinas Powis Castle

FONMON CASTLE   ST 048682

The core of this embattled and rendered mansion with many 18th century sash windows is a keep 13m long by 7.5m wide built by the St John family in the late 12th century but now devoid of medieval features. In the 13th century a court about 17m square was enclosed to the south. Its east wall overlooking a steep slope survives with two small round towers, the northern one adjoining the keep. The southern tower has several original loops and adjoins a square turret projecting from a south range probably built c1320 by Alexander de St John, although it retains no medieval features. Also of that period is a NE tower forming an extension of the older tower adjoining the keep. The St Johns moved to Bletsoe in Bedfordshire after marrying a Beauchamp heiress in the 1420s. A cadet branch stayed in Glamorgan but moved to Highlight. North of the keep is a vaulted cellar of the 1580s, later absorbed into a substantial wing built in 1662 by Philip Jones after his purchase of the castle.

After his marriage to Jane Seys in 1762 Robert Jones had the keep upper room remodelled with a Venetian west window and an east arch towards the space twin towers, where an oriel was provided. Fonmon passed to the Boothby family of Ashbourne in 1917.

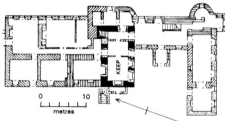

Fonmon Castle

Plan of Fonmon Castle

Fonmon Castle

North gateway at Ewenny Priory

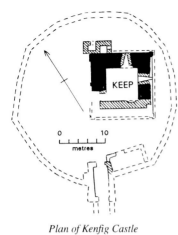

Plan of Kenfig Castle

Remains of the keep at Kenfig

KENFIG CASTLE   SS 802827   F

Excavations in 1924 exposed the lower parts of a tower keep 14m square over walls 3.7m thick with pilaster buttresses at the corners and at the middle of each side. It is thought to have been built by Robert, Earl of Gloucester in the 1140s, in imitation of a larger keep he had already built at Bristol. In 1184 the Welsh destroyed the town and mill and damaged the castle, despite preparations made for an attack, such as the palisading and brattices brought by sea from Chepstow and Bristol. The keep and its surrounding palisade withstood an attack by Morgan Gam in 1232, when the town was again destroyed except for the church. Kenfig was again attacked by the Welsh in 1257, and in 1295 Morgan ap Maredudd succeeded in capturing and burning the keep. The south end wall was then built much thinner and the basement provided with a vault which blocked one of the two loops now remaining. These loops had been inserted in the mid 13th century when two latrines were added on the north side. A curtain wall 1.2m thick above a battered plinth was built to enclose a court about 37m in diameter around the keep, the base of which was partly covered by material then removed from the bailey rampart to make wall for the wall. The only part of the wall now visible above the dunes and vegetation is the eastern impost of the inner arch of the gatehouse on the south side. The castle lay in the north corner of an enclosure 200m square which probably enclosed the town, since it is known to have had earth and timber defences. Thus repaired the castle held out against an attack by Llywelyn Bren in 1316, although its buildings were damaged and the town devastated. In 1321 the castle and town were again ravaged as part of the Marcher lord's campaign against the unpopular Hugh Despenser. Afterwards a short barbican was added to the gatehouse, a building erected in the court east of it, and the keep given a new basement doorway. The castle and town stood at the head of an estuary but the sea has retreated further south and by the 15th century both were becoming inundated with sand-dunes and were abandoned.

Llanblethian Castle

LLANBLETHIAN CASTLE   SS 989743   F

Richard Siward took over the castle in 1233 from the St Quentin family, but he was proclaimed an outlaw by Richard de Clare in 1245 and the castle reverted to de Clare as Lord of Glamorgan. His grandson Gilbert de Clare began rebuilding the castle when he came of age in 1312. It was left incomplete when he was killed at Bannockburn in 1314, and was probably wrecked during the Welsh revolts that followed. The castle was granted to Hugh Despenser in 1317 and again wrecked during the Marcher lords' revolt of 1321 against him. It was finally completed by Edward Despenser, who died at Llanblethian in 1375. The gatehouse remained in use as a prison until the 16th century (when a serving hatch was broken through to the southern room then used as a cell), and was still occupied as a cottage in the 1820s.

Only a 5m high portion of the north wall with a mural stair remains of the 12th century keep of the St Quentins, which was probably about 14 or 15m square. The keep is thought to have originally defended the weakest side of a ringwork 40m across with steep drops from the north, west and south sides. The more ambitious early 14th century court built around the keep has walls up to 2m thick still partly 2m high on the north side, which is 60m long. The west side is also 60m, and there was a turret on the acute-angled corner between them, and the south side is 55m long.

The 40m long east side has low fragments of a rectangular tower 13.5m by 10.5m projecting boldly from the NE corner, the base of a polygonal tower 10m across at the SE corner, and a central gatehouse. Recently consolidated by Cadw, the gatehouse is the best preserved part. It has a passage 3.2m wide flanked by towers 6.4m wide which are polygonal to the field. The tower rooms have crossloops with oillets and doorways opening off the passage, which was closed by a portcullis at either end and a set of doors. At the back of the east tower a set of steps leads up to a spiral stair connecting two upper storeys, the topmost being very ruined. It was a fine chamber connected by the curtain wall-walk 9m above the court to upper rooms in the NE tower. The southern section of wall-walk was at a much lower level.

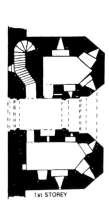

1st STOREY

0 _____ 10
metres

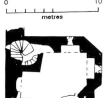

2nd STOREY

Gatehouse plans,
Llanblethian

Llanblethian Castle

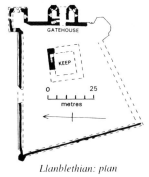

GATEHOUSE

KEEP

0 _____ 25
metres

Llanblethian: plan

West end of Llanblethian Castle

LLANDAFF BISHOP'S PALACE   ST 156780   F

On the ridge SE of the cathedral are ruins of a castle probably built in 1280-7 by Bishop William de Braose. His successors used it until they transferred to Mathern, near Chepstow, in the late 15th century. The decayed walls sheltered the Mathews and the townsfolk during an incursion by Edward Lewis of the Van in 1597. The Mathews had built an adjoining house, and the area within the castle walls later became a garden, although the gatehouse remained inhabited and had the Bush Inn built against it. The land was sold in 1812 but later recovered by the church authorities and in the 1970s the ruins were laid out as a public park.

At the west corner of a court 50m by 35m lies a fine twin-towered gatehouse similar to those of the 1280s at Caerphilly. The towers have spurs rising to chamfered off outer corners facing the field. The 2.4m wide passage was closed by a portcullis and at least one pair of doors. The room NE of it was probably a prison. On the other side was a guard room with a fireplace and four embrasures with crossloops. A stair in an adjoining turret led a pair of upper rooms. The wall-walk on the 2.2m thick north NW curtain wall had a parapet on both sides and led to a hall about 12m long by 7m wide over a basement in a block at the northern corner. A small room in a turret projecting diagonally at the east corner was probably a chapel opening off a solar at the SE end of the hall. One of the two large windows remaining in the outer wall (the only part to survive) lighted this solar.

The 1.9m thick SW wall is 5m high to the wall-walk and has a parapet on a corbel table. The south tower is a square of about 8m containing a basement below court level and two now very ruined upper storeys reached by a straight stair in the curtain wall. A thin modern SE connects it to a circular east tower 5.5m in diameter containing a hexagonal room with a fireplace and two windows over a basement.

Gatehouse at Llandaff Bishop's Palace

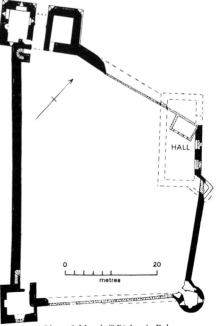

Plan of Llandaff Bishop's Palace

Gatehouse at Llandaff Bishop's Palace

LLANDOUGH CASTLE   SS 995730

Two walls of a 6.5m wide tower with a projecting turret with one ogival-headed trefoiled lancet are incorporated in a building of c1600, itself now part of a house of 1803 built by John Price. The tower lay in the west corner of a court 22m by 28m still partly bounded on the NE side by an overgrown wall 1.3m thick and 4.5m high with fireplaces (mostly blocked) at ground level and latrines in turrets projecting at the east corner and in the middle. A tower 7m by 4m at the south corner has projecting staircase wing where the SW curtain wall adjoined. It was made into a gatehouse c1600 and was restored from a state of dereliction in the 1960s. The Walshes held Llandough from the 12th century until it was sold to Sir William ap Thomas in 1444. The medieval parts were probably built in the 1430s for the heiress Elizabeth Walsh and her husband John de Van. Sir William's descendants sold Llandough to the Carnes in the 1530s and they later remodelled the house. It passed to the Mansels in the 1680s but was let out to a series of tenants, including the Prices, who probably demolished the SE and SW curtain walls.

Main tower at Llandough

SW tower at Llandough

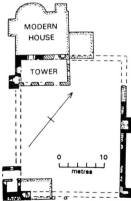

Plan of Llandough Castle

LLANGYNWYD CASTLE   SS 852887

On a strong defensive site on the end of a promontory above a ravine are remains of a wall 2m thick around a D-shaped bailey about 33m across in each direction. Approached by a causeway across a deep rock-cut ditch on the north side is a gateway passage 3.3m wide flanked by D-shaped towers 10m wide and 11m deep. The ground level rooms are probably intact but are currently buried in debris. Enough clearance took place in 1903 to show that the rooms had doorways opening from the passage, which was closed at either end by a portcullis. On the east is a smaller D-shaped tower. There are traces of a barbican beyond the ditch and of an outer bailey extending 50m beyond that. The curtain probably dates from just before the first mention of the castle in 1246, but the earthworks may go back to c1100-20. The castle was captured and wrecked by Llywelyn ap Gruffydd in 1257, twenty four of the garrison being killed. Some repairs were carried out in 1262, before Gilbert de Clare attained his majority. He is assumed to have built the gatehouse c1267-71 as it closely resembles of the gateways then built at Caerphilly. The castle was captured and burnt by Morgan ap Maredudd during the Welsh rebellion of 1295 and was never restored, being referred to in 1307 as "the site of an ancient castle".

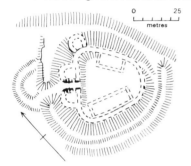

0   25
metres

Plan of Llangynwyd Castle

LLANMAES CASTLE   SS 983694   V

Visible from the road between two houses SE of the church is part of the west end wall of a block 14.5m by 8.5m over walls 1.5m thick. The only feature is a jamb of a basement doorway with a drawbar-slot. It is likely that external steps led to an upper doorway into a hall, perhaps with a solar at the east end. Llanmaes was held by the de Sully family from the 12th century but passed to the Flemings c1331. They probably built the castle, which was held by the Malefants from the 1390s until c1488, and was a ruin by the time of Leland's visit in the 1530s. To the south at SS 980693 hedges mark the line of a moated platform known as Bedford Castle.

LLANQUIAN CASTLE   ST 019745

An overgrown ringwork 18m in diameter on a spur NE of Hollybush Farm on Stalling Down has traces of a masonry revetment and the lower parts of a building about 9m by 7.6m containing a thinly-walled upper room over a vaulted basement. The 2m thick SE wall contained a stair rising from an entrance by the east corner. The St Quentin family held lands here in the 12th century. It passed to Richard Siward of nearby Talyfan but Earl Richard de Clare confiscated these estates in 1245. By 1262 the Nerber family held Llanquain and continued to do so until the 16th century.

Last remaining wall of Llanmaes Castle

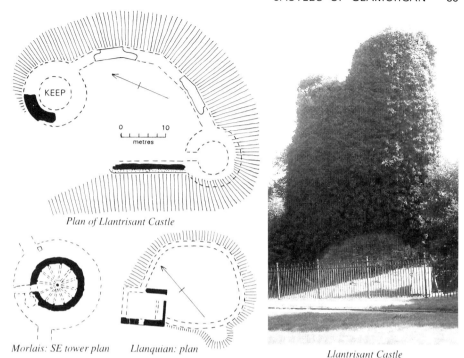

Plan of Llantrisant Castle

Morlais: SE tower plan   Llanquian: plan

Llantrisant Castle

LLANTRISANT CASTLE   ST 047834   F

This castle was built by Richard de Clare in 1246-52 after he had dispossessed the local Welsh ruler Hywell ap Meredudd, although it is thought to lie on the site of a 12th century ringwork. It was wrecked by the Welsh in 1295, damaged during an attack by Llywelyn Bren in 1316, and in 1321 it was one of the Despenser castles captured and wrecked by hostile Marcher lords. Edward II was captured by Queen Isabella's forces nearby. The Raven Tower, probably the keep, was still in use when John Leland saw it c1538. A 13m high ivy-covered fragment remains of a circular keep about 14m in diameter over walls more than 3m thick. Walls 2.4m thick enclosed a D-shaped court extending 24m southwards to where there was a second round tower about 10m across. The length of straight retaining walling above the deep ditch on the west is refaced. Two low fragments of the curtain remain under vegetation on the east and south. Repairs of 1297 seem to have including added a rectangular gatehouse west of the keep, giving a layout not unlike Castell Coch. There are no signs of domestic buildings but there are hints of a large outer ward to the north.

LLANTRITHYD CASTLE   ST 038732

Quarrying has destroyed the western side of a pear-shaped ringwork 55m by 45m. Excavations in the 1960s revealed traces of buildings including an aisled hall in which was a coin hoard from c1122-4. The de Cardiffs held the manor from the early 12th century although they may have later transferred to the moated site of Horseland at ST 042725, where there are footings of a hall on a platform 36m by 30m with a most 8.5m wide on the east. It later passed to the Bassets, and Sir John Basset, d1551, built the now-ruined mansion of Llantrithyd Place nearby.

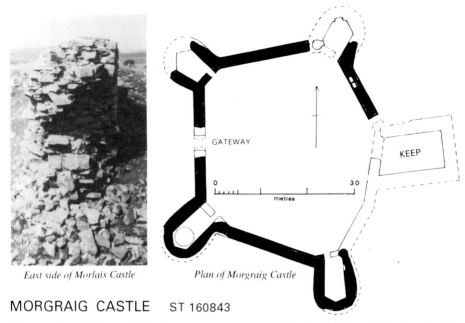

East side of Morlais Castle   *Plan of Morgraig Castle*

MORGRAIG CASTLE   ST 160843

The remains of this castle lie in amongst trees on a ridge beside the A469. Seemingly left incomplete, it was either begun c1260 as a cavalry outpost by Richard de Clare, who died in 1262, or by Gruffydd ap Rhys c1265, who lost the southern part of Senghenydd to Richard's son Gilbert de Clare in 1267. The former is more likely, since cut stones from windows revealed in clearance in 1903 were from districts not under Welsh control, and no other native Welsh castle has such a regular pattern of corner towers. In either case Morgraig was superseded by the castle begun in 1267 at Caerphilly in the valley below. A 2.5m thick curtain wall, still partly 3m high, enclosed a hexagonal court 44m from north to south by 37m wide. The north corners have circular towers 10m across, whilst the southern towers are U-shaped and 14m long. The east corners are covered by a rectangular keep projecting equally boldly towards the top of the ridge. It is 14m wide with a maximum length (the layout is irregular) of 19m, and seems to have had an entrance at ground level like the other towers. A postern adjoins it on the north, beyond which are latrine shoots. The main gateway, now just a breach in the wall, is set between the two western towers.

Morgraig Castle

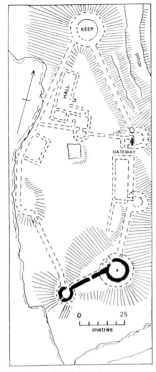

Morlais: plan

Morlais Castle

MORLAIS CASTLE SO 049097 F

On a limestone ridge above the Taff Gorge and the town of Merthyr Tydfil are the last traces of a large and strong castle begun c1287 by Gilbert de Clare on land bounded by that of Humphrey de Bohun, Earl of Hereford. In 1290 a private war broke out between the two earls and they were severely admonished and fined by Edward I, who had to march down from North Wales to intervene. The castle, probably still incomplete, was captured and wrecked in 1294 by Madog ap Llywelyn. It was probably never used again, being too remote and exposed to serve as a lordly residence. The Buck brothers' engraving of 1741, however, shows that fragments of the walls then still stood quite high up.

The castle had a triangular inner court with sides about 45m long at the north end and an outer court extending 60m wide extending 80m to the south. The outer curtain walls were up to 3m thick, although the wall dividing the courts, which had little military function, was much thinner. The inner ward had a huge circular keep at least 18m in diameter at the north corner and contained a hall block 25m long by 9m wide standing isolated on the west side. An adjoining block probably containing private rooms had an apsidal south end projecting beyond the dividing wall between the courts towards a deep cistern pit. East of here lay the inner gateway, and the main outer gateway nearby had a portcullis groove and was guarded by one of two 10m diameter D-shaped towers facing east. Both towers had spiral stairs in their NW corners, where the curtain wall adjoined. The outer ward had no proper towers on the west side, where the ground, now quarried away, was very steep, but the base still remains of a tower about 10m in diameter at the SW corner and the large mound at the SW corner covers the basement of a second huge circular keep about 18m across over walls 5m thick. A passage, originally closed by a portcullis at the courtyard end, and having access to a spiral stair to the lost upper levels, leads to a twelve sided cellar vaulted with ribs radiating from a central pier. Extending from here towards the main outer gateway are traces of two large buildings, perhaps stables. The stone for the castle came from a rock-cut ditch 3m deep lying 12 to 18m away from the walls on the north, east and south sides. Beyond, to the south, a rampart encloses a small southern outer bailey.

East Tower at Neath Castle

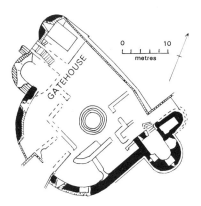

Plan of Neath Castle

Gatehouse at Neath Castle

NEATH CASTLE   SS 754978   F

Earl Robert of Gloucester's constable Richard de Granville had a motte on the west bank of the river, but the site and its lands were donated by him to Neath Abbey at its foundation in 1130. A ringwork probably founded by the earl himself lay on the present site by 1185, when the Welsh attacked it. Rebuilding in stone commenced after it was destroyed by the Welsh in 1231. The garrison drove off Welsh raiders in 1244, and in 1258 withstood a full-scale attack by Llywelyn ap Gruffydd. In 1262-3 the garrison comprised a constable and fifty men, including several servants. The castle withstood attacks during the Welsh revolts of 1314 and 1316 but was captured and wrecked during the rebellion of 1321 against the Despensers. The castle seems to have been repaired by 1324, and further work was done on it in 1377. During the rebellion of Owain Glyndwr the castle held a garrison of over 100 men. It was still tenable in the 1480s, when the constable Richard Willoughby was murdered whilst on his way from the castle to the nearby church, but was presumably abandoned soon afterwards.

Gatehouse at Neath Castle

The gatehouse lies on the west side of a D-shaped court 27m across with the straight side facing north and being flanked by latrine projections adjoining two towers which faced east and west. The east tower is 7.5m wide, 10m long and now stands 5m high. The west tower later became the northern tower of a west-facing gatehouse with a passage 2.8m wide flanked by towers 8m wide and 10m deep. The round outer fronts stand three storeys high and have a high arch with machicolations between them, but the inner parts are reduced to footings. There is a clear contrast between the south tower dating from the 1320s which is U-shaped internally with loops set in embrasures and the older base of the north tower, which is now rectangular internally and has lost its north-facing latrine projection. The upper parts are a 14th century rebuild. Below the 14th century gateway passage are remains of a 13th century postern. The gap on the south is probably the site of the original gatehouse. Excavations in 1970-4 revealed in the courtyard the footings of six 14th century rooms (four of them with fireplaces) arranged around a central square of 11m, within which was an 18th century cockpit and the base of a stair. The short section of walling projecting from the southern tower of the gatehouse is thought to be a relic of a long-forgotten and unrecorded town wall. The early ringwork was accompanied by a bailey which lay to the NW, now a supermarket carpark.

NEWCASTLE BRIDGEND   SS 902801   V

Robert Fitz-Hamon is thought to have had a ringwork here in 1106 marking the western extent of his lordship. The curtain wall 2m thick above a tall battered plinth (now extensively robbed) enclosing a court 40m across was either built by William, Earl of Gloucester shortly before his death in 1183, or by Henry II who then held the lordship of Glamorgan until his own death in 1189, because it was threatened with attack by the Welsh lord of Afan, Morgan ap Caradog. When Prince John took possession of the lordship in 1189 one of his first acts was to hand over Newcastle to Morgan. In c1208 Morgan was succeeded by his son Leison but when he died in 1214 Newcastle reverted to the Countess Isabel, ex wife of King John and heiress of Earl William. From her it passed to Gilbert de Clare but in 1217 he granted Newcastle to Gilbert Turberville of Coity. The Welsh lord of Afan, Morgan Gam claimed Newcastle until he died c1241 but never managed to obtain it either by legal means or by force. Newcastle remained in the same hands as Coity for several centuries and saw little use, although in the mid 16th century John Gamage remodelled the south tower, perhaps to provide accommodation for a steward. The ruin has been in state care since 1932 and is now maintained by Cadw.

The court is polygonal except for having a right-angled SE corner to accommodate an earlier building 10m wide of which footings remain. Footings of a 13th century building lie beyond. The east side has a steep drop down to the River Ogmore, the south side faces the church and the other sides face level ground with modern houses. Two towers 8m square straddle the curtain to strengthen it. That on the south still stands almost 11m high and contains three storeys all with 16th century windows. All the rooms have fireplaces, the top two being original Norman work. Immediately east of this tower is a magnificent gateway arch with a drawbar-slot set in a patch of ashlar where the wall is still 6m high. It has an order of columns with Corinthian capitals carrying a roll-moulded round arch, below which is a segmental inner arch, also roll-moulded with a beaded billet pattern. Nothing remains visible of a tower keep which is said to have stood in the middle of the court.

Gateway at Newcastle Bridgend

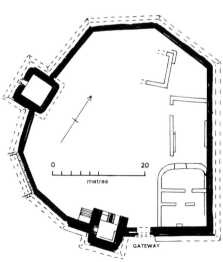

Plan of Newcastle Bridgend

South Tower at Newcastle Bridgend

NORTH CORNELLY: OLD HALL   SS 820816

Hidden away within a modern estate lies the south range of a fortified house probably built c1325-50 by John Luvel, although the windows are 16th and 18th century. Within it are traces of a gateway passage through to a court about 8m square which also had ranges to the west (replaced in the 18th century) and east (now ruined), the latter being the widest (7m externally), so presumably containing the hall. The house later passed to the Turbervilles of Tythegston, who held it until the 18th century.

Internal buildings at Newcastle Bridgend

The keep and gateway at Ogmore Castle

OGMORE CASTLE   SS 882769

Ogmore castle guards a ford with stepping stones over the Ogmore River near its mouth. In 1116 the Welsh forced William de Londres to flee from his castle here, and the keep may have been built as early as c1130 by his son Maurice. A square building of uncertain purpose was erected within the surrounding ringwork by c1180, and then c1210 a hall was built on the north side and a curtain wall 1.2m thick replaced the ringwork bank and palisade. Hawise, heiress of Thomas de Londres, married firstly Walter de Braose in 1223, and then Patrick de Chaworth in 1224. The Chaworths later developed Kidwelly Castle as their main residence and in 1297 their possessions passed by marriage to Henry, younger son of the Earl of Lancaster. Ogmore thus later became part of the duchy of Lancaster merged with the crown since 1399. A carpenter was employed in 1380 to build service rooms in the hall with timber from Neath. The "knighting chamber" (probably the hall) was burnt during Owain Glyndwr's rebellion of 1402-5 and not repaired until the 1440s, although the bridge in front of the gate was repaired in 1429. Leland described the castle in the 1530s as "meatly welle maintainid" but a survey of 1631 indicates that by then only the outer bailey court house remained in use.

The keep measures 14.3m by 9.6m over walls 1.8m thick and originally contained a subdivided upper storey over a dark basement. Only the SW wall remains of the original upper storey, with a fireplace for the inner chamber at the north end and two round-headed windows for the southern chamber. When the 5m high curtain wall was added in the 13th century a turret was created beside the keep NW corner to provide the inner upper chamber and a new chamber created in the old roof space above with latrines. The lowest latrine has a crossloop covering the gateway. The basement of the keep was subdivided by crosswalls in the later medieval period.

The hall on the north side of the ward was 21.7m long by 7.7m wide and lay over a basement lighted only by small loops. Probably the east end was divided off to form a solar about 5.5m wide. Two loops and a doorway with a drawbar slot lie in a portion of the south wall rebuilt in the 15th century. A postern by the hall SE corner was later blocked by a fireplace inserted to serve a room here. The kitchen must have filled most of the corner west of the hall. Projecting from the SE side of the curtain wall are two latrine turrets. Near here is the lower part of a late 12th century building 9.5m by 7.5m over walls 1m thick. Originally the basement was only slightly below the court but material taken with the ringwork rampart when the curtain wall was built was spread around here, raising the level and necessitating extra steps down into the room. On the south side are foundations of a range of offices, and south of the keep is the vaulted entrance passage. Late medieval wing walls extend across the deep dry moat but there is no evidence that the outer bailey to the west had anything other than the still surviving earth ramparts and a palisade. It contains a building thought to be a 14th century court house rebuilt in the 1450s, although the layout of doors and windows makes it possible that it was originally intended as a chapel. Its west end overlies a 13th century lime kiln itself built over an earlier structure. See extra illustration on page 6.

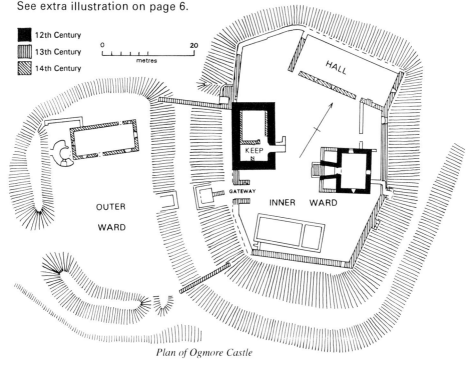

12th Century
13th Century
14th Century

0   metres   20

HALL

KEEP

GATEWAY

INNER   WARD

OUTER
WARD

Plan of Ogmore Castle

PENLLYN CASTLE   SS 979761

Perched on a cliff at the north end of John Homfrey's mansion of c1850 are the NE and NW walls standing 7.5m high of a 12th century keep originally about 12.5m by 8.5m over walls 1.7m thick. The only features are a window with a round rere-arch facing NE, several courses of herringbone masonry on the outer face of the NW side, and an opening in a projection high up towards the east end of that end. This is claimed as an entrance but it looks more like a latrine, especially as the cliff edge is less than 2m away. One would expect an entrance, and any court it faced towards, to be on the destroyed other side of the building. This keep must have been built by Robert Norris, who held the manor by 1135 and lived until c1165. John Norris temporarily had his hands confiscated by Edward II for his part in the rebellion of 1322. In the early 15th century it passed by marriage to Tomkin Turberville. In 1535 Christopher Turberville was wounded during an attack on his house at Penllyn during a feud with Watkin Lougher, as recorded by John Leland. In 1652 Penllyn was described as a "fair house" adjoining a ruined castle. This house fell into decay after being sold in 1703 by the Turbervilles to Richard Seys, and it was derelict by 1786.

PENLLE'R CASTELL   SN 664094   F

Not far east of a high moorland road near Ammanford are remains of what is thought to have been the "New Castle of Gower" burnt by the Welsh in 1252 and then rebuilt in stone. Buried footings of a thinly walled building 8m square lie on a D-shaped platform at the south end. A causeway on the NE connects this with a platform 27m by 20m with a 3.5m deep ditch and traces of second building of similar size.

PENMARK CASTLE   ST 056688   V

In the 12th century Gilbert de Umfraville had a timber castle on this side between the church and a 30m drop into the ravine of the River Waycock. There are footings of several buildings and a projecting tower on the east side of a D-shaped court 55m by 35m. A ditch remains on this side but is filled in on the west where there is a curtain wall 2m thick and 5m high, probably the work of another Gilbert de Umfraville in the 1240s or 50s. His son John perhaps added the D-shaped NW tower 6.5m in diameter now 8m high and the round-cornered latrine projection not far south of it. The lower storey has one complete loop, and the two upper windows have embrasure seats. Both levels have doorways broken through to a small square later extension facing NW, adjoining which is a long thin modern wall extending 60m to where there are remains of a circular dovecote on the rampart of a former outer court. Against the west wall is a ruined barn of c1770. The castle passed by marriage to the St Johns of Fonmon in the early 14th century and probably soon fell into decay.

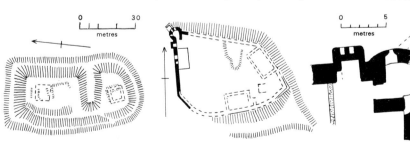

Plan of Penlle'r Castell   *Penmark: plan*   *Penmark: NW tower plan*

Peterston Castle

Penmark Castle

PETERSTON CASTLE   ST 084764   V

The long fragment of 6m high walling in front of Caehir House was the 1.7m thick west wall of a tower 10m long by 7m wide lying at the NW corner of this castle. The fragment is probably early 14th century and contains part of a window and has a latrine chute at the south end. About 38m east of this wall, in the grounds of Castleby, is a smaller and lower fragment of the NW corner of which is thought to have been a gatehouse, south of which are slight traces of a 12th century keep 11.5m wide and probably about 17m long over walls 3m thick, with a latrine chute at the east end. Peterston belonged to the le Sore family from the early 12th century until 1382, when it passed to John Butler from a cadet branch of the le Sores. The keep must have been built either by Odo le Sore c1135-50, or his son John.

RUMNEY CASTLE   ST 210789

The road named Castle Rise cuts through the east part of a former platform 45m by 40m known as Cae Castell lying above the Rhymney River. The platform had a ditch to the east and there was a smaller out platform to the SW. Excavations in 1978-81 revealed two walls of a tower keep 14m by 10m in the NE corner, traces of a gateway on the SE, and parts of other more thinly walled buildings and their timber predecessors. The castle is thought to have been founded by Robert Fitz-Hamon c1100 and to have been strengthened by adding the keep after the revolt of 1184. The manor was handed over by Gilbert de Clare to his mother Maud in 1267 as part of a dower settlement. Her modifications seem to have reduced its defensibility, although the keep still remained. The evidence all suggests it was destroyed by Morgan ap Maredudd in his rebellion of 1294-5 and the site then abandoned.

ST DONAT'S CASTLE   SS 935681

The inner ward was built in the late 12th century by the de Hawey family, who also had estates in Somerset and Dorset. The heiress Joan de Hawey married firstly Sir Peter de Statelynge (Stradling), a Swiss who died c1297, and then secondly John de Pembridge, who rebuilt the castle c1300. It passed to John and Peter's descendants the Stradlings, the last of whom, Sir Thomas, was killed in a duel in France in 1738. In the late 14th century Sir Edward was twice sheriff of Glamorgan, and his grandson Edward married a daughter of Henry VI's great-uncle Cardinal Beaufort and became Chamberlain of South Wales in 1423. He died on a pilgrimage to the Holy Land in 1453, four years after his son Henry was captured by pirates whilst crossing over from Somerset and had to be ransomed for 1000 marks. This Henry must have later remodelled the hall and added the Gibbet Tower, and his grandson Sir Edward, d1535, rebuilt the north and west ranges. John Stradling was made a baronet by James I in 1611 despite being the family being Catholic. They fought for King Charles in the Civil War and a Stradling led the Royalist force defeated in 1648 at St Fagans. Subsequently they declined to the status of local gentry. In 1738 the estates passed to Bussey, 4th Baron Mansell of Margam, after whose death they were divided, St Donats going to Sir John Tyrrwhitt in 1755. The castle was later neglected until sold in 1862 to a Stradling descendant, Dr Nicholl Carne, who began its restoration. The castle was sold in 1801 to Morgan Stuart Williams, who sought a refuge from the squalor of his coalmines at Aberpergwm. It was sold in 1922 to Richard Pennoyer, but in 1925 he resold it to a fellow American, the newspaper millionaire William Randolph Hearst, for whom it was remodelled, using quite a number of old parts from other buildings. The castle was commandeered for training army officers during the war and in 1962 was taken over by an international school called Atlantic College.

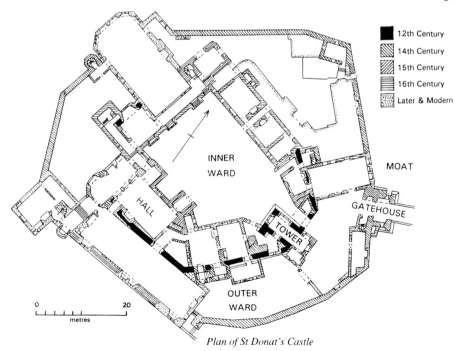

Plan of St Donat's Castle

St Donat's Castle

The castle originally consisted of a single court about 40m across with a wall 1.2m thick and 4.5m high with a tower 10m by 6.5m projecting within the court alongside its east facing gateway. The castle lies on the end of a promontory with a sheer drop to the west, an unlikely site for a concentric castle, yet in the early 14th century this is what it came. Just 10m to 12m away from the inner wall was built an outer wall with a gatehouse on the east, where there is a rock-cut ditch, and one small internally projecting tower in the north corner. All the 14th century parts have parapets on corbel-tables. The gatehouse has a portcullis operated from an upper room with trefoiled lancets, reached by a spiral stair on the south side. There is a coat of arms under an upper blind arch over the outer archway. Beside the gatehouse is an Elizabethan brewhouse. Circulation of the outer ward is now interrupted in three places. Just north of the inner and outer gateways a 16th century range straddles the ward. On the NW is the Dining Hall ending in a bow front beyond the outer curtain wall which towers over the cliff-edge. On the south side the Bradenstoke Hall was created in the 1920s, its SE corner causing a breach in the outer curtain wall, and its roof a 14th century piece from the priory of Bradenstoke. The big fireplace in it is French 16th century work. North of this hall is the 15th century hall, a room 12m by 8m with a porch at the NE corner and a bay window at the other end. The other ranges in the inner ward are also 15th and early 16th century and on the north and west little remains of the original inner curtain wall. In the NW corner is the rectangular 15th century Gibbet tower, with three upper storeys linked by a spiral stair in a turret on the south side. Some of the busts in roundels in the court may be 16th century. The 14th century remodelling of the inner ward included adding a round tower 8m in diameter at the SW corner, providing a gateway and the lengthening of the Mansell Tower beside it eastward towards the outer ward. This tower retains one blocked Norman window on the north and has a deeply battered base. The lofty Lady Anne tower at the SW corner of the outer ward is of the 1930s, incorporating reset windows from a smaller 16th century tower here. See extra illustrations of the castle on pages 3, 9 and 11.

Postern at St Fagans Castle

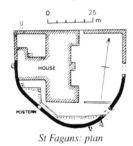

St Fagans: plan

ST FAGANS CASTLE   ST 120772   O

On a bluff above the Ely River is a D-shaped court measuring 57m by 47m which is surrounded by a curtain wall 2m thick, the curved southern part being 13th century work. The ditch on the east and north sides has been filled in and the only medieval feature is a narrow pointed postern doorway on the SW which was reopened in 1947 after being blocked up for centuries. Peter le Sore probably erected a ringwork here after dispossessing the Welsh lord Meurig ap Hywell in 1091. In the early 14th century the castle passed by marriage to the le Vele family, and in 1475 it passed to David Mathew upon his marriage to the heiress Alice le Vele. The descendants of their daughters sold the castle to Dr John Gibbon c1560, and in 1586 it was purchased by Nicholas Herbert of Cogan Pill, who squared off the NE corner of the court, built a new mansion inside it, and laid out the walled garden to the north. The castle was sold again in 1616 to Sir Edward Lewis of The Van, near Caerphilly. In 1730 the Windsor 3rd Earl of Plymouth married the heiress Elizabeth Lewis. Some internal work was undertaken in the 1760s but by 1815 the castle was neglected and used only by a farmer. In was restored in the 1850s, and in 1946 was presented to the National Museum of Wales, the grounds being opened as a folk museum in 1948.

ST GEORGES CASTLE   ST 099768

Castle Farm is a 15th century house built by the Malefants on the remains of a castle built either by the de Sully family or Sir William Fleming, who married the de Sully heiress c1316, and was executed at Cardiff in 1322. The thick west and north walls of the lower storey probably contain older work, and the north wall overlooks a steep drop to the River Ely. The house was later held by the Herbert earls of Pembroke.

SULLY CASTLE   ST 152683

Excavations in 1963-9, before the site was built upon, found traces of a ringwork about 55m in diameter, into the bank of which on the north side was inserted a stone keep 19m long by 11.5m wide with a projection containing a cess-pit the NE end, where the wall was 3.6m thick. The side walls seem to have been 2.7m thick and the SW wall was 2.1m thick. In the 14th century a hall block was built SE of the keep and a court formed east of it. All these buildings were contained in a new outer wall 1.5m thick enclosing a court 65m by 60m, basically nearly square but with the south side bowed out. There were towers about 10m by 6m lying entirely within the northern corners, and a west facing gateway just south of the NW tower. This castle was held by the de Sully family, the earliest member on record being Walter in the period 1190-1214. In the 14th century it passed to the de Braose family and then c1350 was purchased by the Despenser lord of Glamorgan. It was later abandoned in favour of the moated site at Middleton on Sully Moors 500m to the north at ST 093720, where there are slight traces of a platform 30m by 27m.

TRECASTELL ST 016814 V

William Scurlage is thought to had a fortified house here in the mid 13th century. It is mentioned under the name Scurlage Castle in 1320, when it was held by the Despensers. Incorporated in a 16th century barn are parts of the 1.4m thick south wall (built on a rock outcrop), and west wall (facing a steep drop) of a court about 25m square. From the 15th century until modern times the Gibbon family held the estate, which has been known as Trecastell since the late 16th century, when George Gibbon is assumed to have built the house in the northern part of the court demolished in 1967 to make way for various farmyard buildings and enclosures.

TREODA MOTTE ST 156804

This motte in the manor of Whitchurch was reduced in height in the 19th century and finally destroyed to make way for development in 1966 after excavations had shown it was raised over a Bronze Age barrow. It lay on the east side of a former Roman fort, about 60m east of the footings of the medieval church, and the 19th century mansion also removed in 1966 stood on the site of a medieval house. The antiquary G.T.Clark was told by the owner in 1848 that stonework recently removed from the mound included ashlar and evidence of a gateway with a portcullis groove.

OTHER MEDIEVAL FORTIFIED SITES IN GLAMORGAN

BONVILSTON ST 071734 Oval ringwork 36m by 30m on low lying site. Seat of Bonville family from mid 12th century until given to Margam Abbey c1250.

BRITON FERRY SS 731940 Traces of ditch on rocky knoll west of river may indicate site of castle built c1180 by Morgan ap Caradog ab Iestyn, Lord of Afon.

BRYNWELL ST 147744 Traces of oval platform 30m across by farm.

CADOXTON ST 128688 Last remains of 14th century stronghouse of the Andrew family, owners until 1683, were cleared away after a new house was built to the south in 1873. Beyond, on edge of slope, is a circular medieval dovecote.

CAE GARN ST 184850 Low mound on possible site of medieval beacon tower.

CAERAU ST 135751 Ringwork 45m by 37m with rampart 3m high set near ruined church in NE corner of Iron Age hillfort. Manor held by bishops of Llandaff.

CASTELL BOLAN SS 768920 Small mound, possibly altered, on promontory.

CASTELL NOS SN 965001 Rocky knoll fortified by the Welsh with ditch.

COED-Y-CYM ST 083737 Ringwork 33m across with rampart 3m above ditch.

COGAN HALL ST 169705 Probably on site of unrecorded castle of de Cogan family.

COSMESTON ST 176689 Road has obliterated west side of a walled and moated court 22m square, possibly a 13th century stronghouse of the de Constantines. Dovecote base revealed by 1982 excavation in garden enclosure further west.

COTTRELL ST 081745 Mound rising 2.5m from ditch to summit 21m across.

CWRT-YR-ALA ST 139734 Enclosure about 30m square with rampart and ditch on sloping site. Possible tower in SW corner and two buildings within court.

DUNRAVEN SS 888728 Medieval clifftop castle of Butlers passed to the Vaughans. No medieval remains, nor does much survive of Dunraven family's house of 1802.

FELIN ISAF ST 061793 Mound rising 3m to irregularly shaped summit 20m across and slight traces of bailey 35m by 30m to NW.

GELLIGAER ST 137969 Steep sided mound called Twyn Castell east of church is 6m high on east, but only 3m high on west. Summit 18m across.

GELLI-GARN SS 960787 Ringwork 25m across with ditch and bailey to east, probably demilitarised after given to Neath Abbey in 1150s.

GWERN-Y-DOMEN ST 175879 Ringwork 25m across in marsh by railway.

LLANCAEACH FAWR ST 113967 Stronghouse of three storeys and attic erected c1520-30 by Richard ap Lewis or his son David. Only entrance has drawbar slot.

LLANDOUGH ST 169732 House near church on site of possible motte or ringwork.

LLANDOW SS 942732 Slight ditch 120m SW of church. Corner of building found.

LLANGEWYDD SS 875810 Dismantled after being given to Neath Abbey by David Scurlage c1210. No earthworks or building now remain.

LLANILID 978813 Treeclad ringwork 30m across on top and 4.5m high.

MARCROSS SS 923692 Slight remains around farmyard of thinly walled SE and SW ranges of a fortified house probably built in 14th century be the de Beres, but later held by the de Vans of Llantwit Major and abandoned when male line ended 1695. Part of SW wall and mound on site of possible south corner tower removed c1980.

MARSH HOUSE ST 030667 Court of 1636 30m by 20m with wall 2.4m high and 0.6m thick pierced with musket loops. Loop in projecting store guarded gateway. Slightly later house at other end of court. Gone, site buried under ash-heaps.

MORGANSTOWN ST 1128819 Mound rising 4m from wet ditch to summit 13m across with 40m square bailey to east with low east rampart.

OLDCASTLE BRIDGEND SS 905795 Supposed site of castle. Loop base in barn.

OLDCASTLE-UPON-ALUN SS 911748 Probable site of castle with a court about 60m in diameter with traces of ditch on NW and steep drop on the NE.

PANCROSS ST 047700 Slight traces of ringwork 30m across with bailey 55m by 45m to west. Probably a castle of the de Umfravilles.

PEN-Y-PIL ST 227803 Platform 33m across with marsh to south and rampart and ditch to north. 12th century pottery found in excavation of 1965.

RUPERRA ST 223867 Motte rising 6m to summit 12m across with ditch and outer bank set near NE end of hillfort so as to leave 40m long bailey beyond.

ST NICHOLAS GAER ST 085748 Ringwork 52m by 44m rising 5m above ditch.

STORMY SS 846815 Damaged mound 3m high with top 16m across. Seat of de Sturmi family in mid 12th century.

TOMEN-Y-CLAWYDD ST 092865 Mound rising 4m from ditch with outer bank to summit 22m across lying in housing estate. Free access.

TWMPATH (RHIWBINA) ST 154822 Mound rising 6m to summit 15m across.

TY DU ST 046771 Mound 1.5 high with wet ditch and summit 12m across.

TYTHEGSTON COURT SS 857789 Turberville tower 6m by 7m with part of hall-block at north end. No medieval features remain. Set at SW corner of Loughor family's 16th century mansion remodelled (& rendered) in 1760s by Henry Knight.

VAYNOR SO 047102 Small mound high above Taf Fechan opposite Morlais Castle.

WALTERSTON S068712 Part of rampart of ringwork. Ditch recently filled in. Base of mortared building alongside. Traces of large enclosure to north.

WENVOE ST 119713 No remains of the medieval castle of the de Sullys, later held by the Flemings and Malefants, nor of Edmund Thomas's mansion of c1600 on the same site, replaced by mansion of 1776-7 mostly demolished after fire in 1910.

WRINSTON ST 135726 14th century stronghouse of de Ralegh family "al in ruin saving one high tower" when seen by Leland c1538. Farmbuildings on site.

YNYSCRUG SS 995928 Fragment of west side of mound by Rhonnda River. Mostly destroyed in 1855 for railway. Traces of bailey to south now gone.

YSTRADOWEN ST 011777 Unfinished motte 5m high. Intended top 20m across.

SELECTED MOATED SITES IN GLAMORGAN (See also p82 & p96)

CAERWIGAU ST 057754, COITY HIGHER SS 914824, FELINDRE SS 972813
GADLYS SS 979811, HIGHLIGHT* ST 100697, LIEGE CASTLE ST 054734
LLYSWORNEY SS 962743, MAENDY BACH ST 064785, MIDDLETON ST 151687
MICHAELSTON COURT ST 119764, WORLETON ST 093720   (* - excavated)

LANDIMOR CASTLE   SS 464933

On a shelf above the marshes lie ruins of a hall block with courts north and south of it, the north court also having east and west domestic ranges. Traces remain of a wall 2m thick and 60m long with towers at each end protecting the vulnerable west side. The castle is assumed to be the work of Sir Hugh Johnys, c1452-85. By 1500 it passed to Sir Rhys ap Thomas and was abandoned in favour of adjoining Weobley.

LOUGHOR CASTLE   SS 564980   F

Henry de Villers, Steward of Gower under Henry, Earl of Warwick probably raised a ringwork here c1106 in the NE corner of the Roman fort guarding the mouth of the River Loughor and the west approach to Gower. This was probably the castle in Gower destroyed by Gruffydd ap Rhys of Deheubarth before his assault upon that at Swansea in 1116. It also seems to have been captured and burnt by the Welsh in 1136 and 1151. By 1215, when all the castles of Gower, including Loughor, were captured by Rhys ap Gruffydd, the lordship had passed to the de Braose family. Reginald de Braose briefly recovered Gower in 1217 but it was occupied by the Welsh until 1220, when Llywelyn ab Iorwerth came to terms with Henry III. Reginald's nephew John is then thought to have built an ovoid shell wall 1.6m thick around a court measuring 25m by 19m with a north facing entrance and a tower on the west side. This tower was later replaced by the present structure, perhaps by John Iweyn, Steward of Gower under the third William de Braose, by whom he was granted Loughor in 1302. He was captured and executed at Swansea by the rebel barons in 1321, being as a hated official of the unpopular Hugh Despenser. The castle then reverted to the lordship of Gower and was probably left to decay. Leland didn't comment on its condition but Merrick described it as ruinous in 1587.

The surviving tower measures 8m by 7.2m and guarded a new gateway immediately south of it. Over a basement (with a drawbar slot in its doorway) were two upper rooms each with two crudely made lancet windows, a fireplace in the north wall, and a latrine in the south wall. The middle room was reached by a straight stair from the court and than a spiral stair in the SE corner led to the top room. The rooms were quite low and the wall-walk was only about 7.5m above the courtyard.

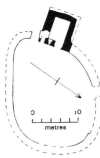

Loughor: plans   *Loughor Castle*

OXWICH CASTLE   SS 497863

Philip Mansel had a castle at Oxwich in 1459, the Mansells having obtained the manor (which belonged to the de la Meres until the 13th century) by marriage to a Penrice heiress. The south range, the west facing gateway, and the dovecote on the north side are the work of Sir Rice Mansel, probably of c1520-35. The huge east range was the work of his son Sir Edward, who inherited in 1559 and lived until 1585. However it incorporates part of a late medieval hall range. The ivy-clad structure perched on a rock within woodland 85m NE of the castle is sometimes described as being an earlier medieval tower here, although its nature (a single room 92m by 42m within walls 1.1m thick with small openings) is more that of a chantry chapel but for the fact that it is aligned north-south rather than east-west. Sir Rice Mansel had purchased the Margam Abbey estate in 1540 and by the 17th century the family resided there, and Oxwich was leased out. During the 18th century the east range fell into ruin although the south range is still roofed. After World War II the site was purchased by Lady Apsley and placed in state guardianship.

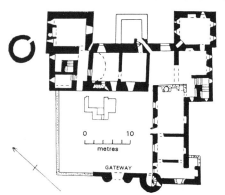

A gateway with twin round turrets and archway surmounted by an armorial panel and a machicolation leads into a court 20m by 16. The south range has two upper rooms (now thrown into one) with fireplaces on the south and four-light windows facing north. The windows of the lower level are not ancient. A conical-roofed turret at the NW corner contains a spiral stair connecting the upper and lower storeys and an attic, and also gives out onto the wall-walk on the west curtain wall.

Plan of Oxwich Castle

Oxwich Castle from the SW

NE tower at Oxwich

Oxwich Castle

The east range is a most impressive structure 9.7m wide over walls up to 2m thick at the level of the two vaulted cellars under the hall. Here older masonry may survive although the vaults and openings all appear to be late 16th century. A porch in the court contained steps up to the north end of a hall 17m long by 7m wide and 8m high. One six light west window is blocked. Another further south, which extended down to floor level, is now blocked. The south end projecting beyond the older south range contained three storeys of private rooms linked by a scale-and-platt staircase in the SE corner, and having bedrooms in a six storey embattled tower projecting east towards the sea. Over the hall and these chambers was a long gallery extending the whole 32.5m internal length of the building. North of the hall was a lobby and then a second scale-and-platt staircase linking the bedrooms over a kitchen in another six storey tower facing east at this end, whilst smaller rooms were tucked into the NW corner beside the stair. Only the footings remain of a third intermediate eastern tower. The bedrooms mostly have fireplaces and single-light windows fitted with hoodmoulds and seats in the embrasures.

OYSTERMOUTH CASTLE   SS 613883   O

There are no certain early references to this castle, but the central keep must predate when William de Braose became Lord of Gower in 1203. It was remodelled and another block added on the north side after the building was burnt by the Welsh in 1215. A thinly walled NW wing was added later and the curtain walls were probably built after the castle was destroyed by Llywelyn ap Gruffydd when he over-ran Gower in 1257. Edward I spent two days at the castle as the guest of the second William de Braose in 1284, but three years later it was again captured by the Welsh under Rhys ap Maredudd. The third William de Braose, d1326, later added the impressive SE block containing the chapel. The castle passed to the Mowbrays in 1331. They lost possession to the Beauchamps in 1354, after a legal battle, but recovered it in 1397. Neither they, nor the Herberts who succeeded them as Lords of Gower, used the castle much and it probably fell into decay. Either during this period or during the Civil War of the 1640s the drum towers of the gatehouse were removed. Parliament granted the castle to Oliver Cromwell but it was recovered later by the Dukes of Beaufort, who were descended from the Herberts. The ruin was patched up in the 1840s (when the tracery of the chapel windows was restored) and sold to the Borough of Swansea in 1927.

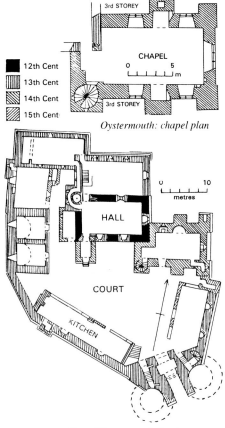

■	12th Cent
▥	13th Cent
▧	14th Cent
▨	15th Cent

Oystermouth: chapel plan

Chapel block at Oystermouth

Plan of Oystermouth Castle

The gatehouse at Oystermouth

The lower part of the original keep 16.8m by 10m over walls 1.7m thick set on a rock outcrop with a small bailey north of it, and an outer bailey to the east, was remodelled in the 1200s as the southern part of a central block containing a hall and chamber of equal size side by side on each of two storeys, where there were fireplaces back-to-back in the spine wall. The chambers both retain lancets in embrasures with seats and below them the fall of the ground allows a vaulted cellar which was reached by a spiral stair directly from the upper hall NW corner. The upper and lower halls were separately reached from the outside by early 14th century porches set one above the other at the SW corner. The porch doorways have drawbar slots and the lower one has a machicolation. From the lower hall a passage is taken round the NW spiral stair without a doorway to it and through the west wall of the lower chamber to give access to a barrack room in a mid 13th century north-west wing 16m long. Below the barrack room were two levels of storage, the lowest vaulted originally, the upper as part of later alterations, and there was another chamber above. Cisterns were divided off at the west end of the barrack room.

A late 13th century block lies south of the NW wing and connects it with an another mid 13th century block further south later remodelled to provide two upper rooms over two vaulted cellars. Opening off the SE corner of the upper hall in the central block is a fine chapel with cusped intersecting tracery in windows of two and three lights, a piscina and recesses set in buttresses set on each side. The three unengaged corners of this lofty early 14th century block are clasped by square turrets, that at the SW containing a spiral stair, and that at the SE containing latrines serving the two levels of chambers below. There are also mid-wall buttressed on the long sides. There are ruinous late medieval service ranges on the south and east sides of the court. The gateway passage was closed with a portcullis and two sets of doors and is flanked by long passages with steps which once led to circular guard rooms in the bases of drum towers about 7m in diameter. One passage gives onto a stair to the upper storey and wall-walk. When the outer parts of the drums were removed the entrance passage was extended slightly outwards but the joist holes of the floors of the tower upper rooms were left open.

Pennard Castle

PENMAEN CASTLE   SS 534880   F

The end of a headland on the west side of Pennard Pill is cut off by a rampart 6m high with a ditch in front to make an oval court 38m long by 27m wide. Excavations in 1960-1 revealed the post-holes of a wooden gate tower 6m square that was burnt in a Welsh attack and replaced by a narrower entrance of unmortared stone. Also found were low drystone walls of a hall on the south side measuring 12.5m by 5m internally. The Harengs are thought to have lived here until expelled in 1217.

PENNARD CASTLE   SS 545885   F

Excavations in 1961 found traces of a ringwork possibly first established here c1110 by Henry de Beaumont, Earl of Warwick. Footings of a drystone hall block were then also revealed on the west side of the court. The castle is first mentioned in 1322 when Hugh Despenser was given a royal licence to obtain the castles of the lordship of Gower by an exchange of lands, and it had then recently been rebuilt in stone. The lands and the adjacent church were overcome by sand-dunes but the castle probably remained in use until the end of the medieval period since a Buck brothers engraving of 1741 shows the ruined buildings as almost complete.

Pennard Castle

Penmaen: plan

Pennard Castle

The D-shaped court perched high above the east side of Pennard Pill measures 33m by 27m within a wall 1.2m thick. It is best preserved above the cliff on the north, and there is a small D-shaped turret at the NW corner. SW of this is a late medieval square building now about 3m high built out on a platform outside the west curtain, which is there 5m high to a wall-walk so thin that a timber platform would have been needed to make use of it. Most of the parapet also still survives. On the south side only one 6m long section of the curtain still stands, with at its east end a hint of another round turret or tower. On the east side is a gatehouse still partly standing to its original height of about 11m. It had towers 4.5m wide and 6.4m deep flanking a passage 2.4m wide closed by a portcullis, the grooves of which did not descend to ground level, making it very weak. A doorway with a drawbar slot on the north side led into a single upper room with a loop in each of the tower fronts and at least one loop facing the court, and there were guardrooms with loops below.

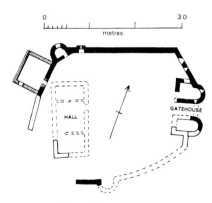

Plan of Pennard Castle

Solar block at Penrice

PENRICE CASTLE   SS 498885 & 492879

The ringwork called Mounty Brough SW of the church is the site of the earliest castle of the Penres family. Now very overgrown, and measuring 42m by 30m it has a rampart rising 3m above the land to the east and 6m high above the ditch with a counterscarp bank on the west. After his marriage in 1237 Robert de Penres transferred to the site on the other side of the ravine north of the church, building a round tower keep and a curtain wall to enclose a D-shaped court 85m by 55m on the end of a promontory. A long barn was provided on the NE side. Later on Robert added the gatehouse, and then in the 1280s or 90s, after the Welsh threat receded, another Robert de Penres, probably his son, built a hall-block with twin projecting wings over the site of the SW end of the landward-facing curtain wall.

A later Robert de Penres, who married into the powerful de Camville family, incurred the wrath of Edward III in 1362 when his Welsh castles were reported to be ruinous. His estates were forfeited in 1377 when he was convicted of the murder of a woman at Llanstephan back in 1370. His son repurchased the estate but left no heirs, and in the early 15th century Penrice passed to the Mansels of Oxwich. Sir Rice Mansel let the castle to William Benet, whose heirs resided in it until 1669. The landward defences may have suffered some dismantling during the Civil War. It was a total ruin when engraved by the Buck brothers in the early 18th century and in the 1770s Thomas Mansel Talbot built a new house down below it to the south.

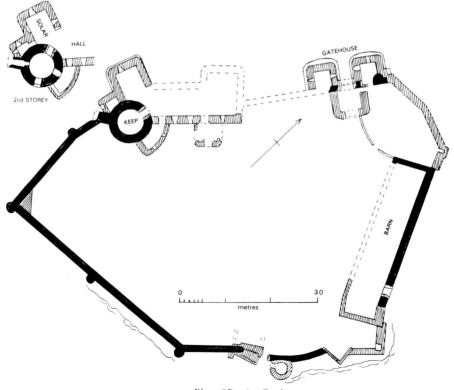

Plan of Penrice Castle

Gatehouse at Penrice

Penrice is the largest castle on the Gower peninsular and has a number of unusual features. The keep, gatehouse and much of the curtain wall still stand up high but in a dangerous and ivy-clad state. The keep measures 9.7m in diameter over walls 2.1m thick and contained a single room with three windows and a latrine over an unlit basement. It was later heightened but the topmost level has no openings of any kind. In front of the upper doorway was added a flat-roofed chemise with a parapet facing the court. On the other side of the keep is a square block with round corners which contained over an unlit basement a solar with a fireplace, two windows and access to a latrine in a turret on the west side (see page 105). Of a hall on the upper storey of an adjacent range only the inner wall survives together with fragments of a later medieval porch. The block must have contained further rooms in its NE end, where another tower-like wing projected out. The total destruction of the outer walls here, and the curtain wall as far as the gatehouse looks like mid 17th century slighting. The three storey gatehouse has a block about 8m square within the court and a pair of 7m square towers with rounded outer corners projecting towards the field. The passage has a portcullis groove. No stairs remain and there seems to have been an external stair to a doorway on the NE side of the inner part of the gatehouse. The curtain wall round the cliff edge is from 1.6m to 2m thick and has tiny circular turrets at the SW corner and on the west and south sides. A fourth turret on the south has recently collapsed. The NE tower of the gatehouse is built against a fifth turret, the late medieval dovecote on the SE probably replaces a sixth, and two more on the east are likely to have existed. There are latrines in sections of the curtain wall rebuilt later at the northern and eastern corners, the later now projecting as a salient.

SALT HOUSE, PORT EYNON SS 467846 F

The low walls exposed here in 1986-7 are those of a boiling house for collecting salt from seawater, but indications were found that it had later been adapted as a stronghouse. It is said to have been used by the Lucas family, notorious smugglers who are alleged to have hidden contraband in Culver Hole, a tower-like 14th century dovecote dramatically set in a cleft in the cliffs a short distance round to the west (at SS 465846). The dovecote served a stone castle of Port Eynon above it, which is mentioned in 1353, but which has been quarried away. The estate passed from the de la Meres to the Penres family in the 14th century and later went to the Mansels.

SWANSEA CASTLE   SS 657931   V

When the large block of buildings on the east side of Castle Street were erected in 1913 on the site of Henry de Newburgh's motte of c1106 evidence was found of destruction by fire, probably a relic of the Welsh attack of 1116, when only the keep survived unharmed. A curtain wall around a court about 38m by 60m with one square tower on the west side was probably added either by William, Earl of Warwick, or by Henry II after he took the lordship of Gower into his own hands in 1184. William de Londres was besieged in the castle by Rhys ap Gruffydd for ten weeks in 1192 before a relief force arrived from England. In 1203 King John granted Gower to William de Braose. The two later fell out and in 1210 William's son William and wife Matilda were starved to death by the king at Windsor. As a result Swansea was in royal hands when it was attacked by the Welsh in 1212. Twenty marks was spent on strengthening the castle that year, and its defences were tested again in other Welsh attacks led by Rhys Ieuanc in 1215 and 1217. Rhys Grug held Gower until 1220 and some time after its return to John de Braose a large outer bailey, enclosing the inner bailey and measuring 100m by 150m was walled in stone.

It was probably after Rhys ap Meredudd had captured the town and castle in a surprise attack in 1295 that the present building was laid out in the SE corner of the outer bailey and the inner bailey on the motte seems to have been abandoned. In 1317 and 1338 murage grants were issued to help pay for town walls of which nothing now survives. The castle passed to the Mowbrays in 1331. They rarely visited Gower yet for some reason the new hall and chamber were adorned with arcaded parapets in the mid 14th century. As a result of a court judgement Gower was led by the earls of Warwick from 1354 until 1397, when the Mowbrays recovered it. Swansea Castle was provisioned and repaired in the expectation of an attack by Owain Glyndwr in 1402-3, although there is no record of one. In the 1460s Edward IV entrusted Sir William ap Herbert to govern Gower, and the gunports in the top of the round tower date from that period. During the 16th century the castle mainly served as a prison. A town hall is said to have been erected on the west side of the courtyard. The town and castle were garrisoned by the Royalists during the Civil War. There is no evidence of a siege but the castle seems to have been made indefensible by order of Parliament in 1647. A survey of 1650 notes the hall-block as being decayed and after refers to the ruins of the older inner ward further north, whilst the Buck brothers' engraving of 1741 shows a motte bare of masonry between the later building and other medieval walls still remaining north of it.

NE tower at Swansea

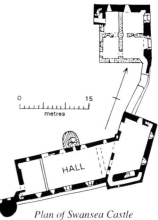

Plan of Swansea Castle

The castle lies above what was once a steep slope down to the River Tawe. The town extended in a L-shape to the west and south of the castle and had gates facing north (across the High Street), east (across Wind Street), and to the SW, SE and west. Part of the town wall, with one tower, was discovered during building work in 1925.

The existing ruin or "newerke" set in the outer bailey SE corner dates from about 1300, except that the remarkable arcaded parapets (similar others on the palaces of the Bishop of St Davids) are additions of the 1340s or 50s, the D-shaped stair-turret on the NW side of the hall block is 15th century, and there are traces of later alterations, the solar block having once contained the furnaces of a glass works. The main block contained a lofty hall 12m long by 7.5m wide and a service area at the SW end set over three vaulted cellars each with one cross-loop with four oillets towards the field and a doorway from the court. One cellar is linked with the hall by a spiral stair in an added turret. The hall had two windows on either side and a doorway with a drawbar slot approached from a court 3m below the present level by means of a staircase in a porch. A spiral stair from the service area led to a room above it. The solar lay over two rooms with a cellar beneath them and had a triangular lobby between it and the hall because the two ranges meet at an obtuse angle. The later arcading carries a wall-walk with a corbelled parapet with loops with top and bottom oillets, and the solar south end is carried up as a turret. At the same time a latrine turret backing onto the curtain wall west of the wall (where there was probably a kitchen) was given two upper levels set on corbelling, the lower level having foiled lancets and the upper 15th century gunloops. A thick length of curtain wall leads from the solar to a two storey block to the north which remained in use as a prison until 1853. It measures 12.4m by 10.4m and has a modern concrete top over four cells set over a vaulted basement. West of it was a curtain wall 2m thick and 8m high.

The arcaded parapet at Swansea Castle

The hall block at Swansea

TALYBONT CASTLE   SN 587027

The ditched mound now overlooking a cutting of the M4 is thought to have been raised c1106 by Henry de Villers who owed the service of two knights (one for here and one for Loughor) at the Lord of Gower's castle at Swansea. Hugh de Meules held this castle in 1215, when it was destroyed by Rhys Ieuanc. It appears that the site remained in use until the mid 14th century, when it had reverted to the lords of Gower, but there are no signs of masonry on the mound, which rises 6m to an oval summit 10m by 15m. There are slight traces of a bailey 50m wide to the south.

WEOBLEY CASTLE   SS 478928   C

Weobley Castle is first mentioned in 1318 and was probably begun by David de la Bere in 1304. The building shows clear signs of having been completed to a more modest scale than that originally laid out and further modifications followed the period of Owain Glyndwr's revolt of 1402-5, after which the castle was described as a fortified manor house ("manorium battellatum") recently destroyed by the Welsh. The de Bere male line failed in the mid 15th century and Weobley passed successively to the St Johns, the Bassets, and then to Sir Rhys ap Thomas, who carried out much work on the castle in the 1490s. His son Gruffydd assigned Weobley to his spouse Lady Katherine St John. The lands went to the Crown when she died in 1553 because her son Rhys had been attainted and executed for treason in 1531. Lady Katherine let the building to a tenant, a practice continued by the subsequent owners under whom the building degenerated into a partly inhabited farmhouse. Elizabeth I sold Weobley in 1560 to William Herbert, Earl of Pembroke, and the 5th Earl of Pembroke sold it to Sir Edward Mansel of Margam in 1666. By then a new farmhouse stood beside the abandoned castle.

Weobley from the NE

Weobley Castle

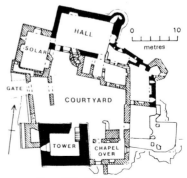

Plan of Weobley Castle

West side of Weobley Castle

The castle lies on the edge of a steep drop to the marshes on the north side of Gower. The earliest parts are a hall block on the north side and a tower house on the south side. The southern half of the east range with a SE latrine tower was never built above the foundations, and against the hall block are toothings for an intended solar block. The hall block measures 14m by 9.6m over walls 1.4m thick. Originally perhaps of just one storey, as completed c1320-40 it had a hall with a single window embrasure in each of the east and south walls above a kitchen with three north windows. A stair in a circular NE turret led from the hall to the battlements. About the same time the northern part of the east range was completed and a polygonal latrine turret added at the NE corner. A block 10.5m by 7.5m containing a solar with a fireplace, SW corner latrine, and three windows over a cellar which was later subdivided, was then added SW of the hall. South of the solar is a 5.4m wide range which contained the gateway, protected by a dry moat in front but closed only by a two-leaved door in a thin outer wall. Of the 1490s are the porch in front of the hall, the stair turret west of it, and a block containing extra rooms to the east of it.

The tower house measures 10m by 8.4m over walls 2m thick. The basement has a north doorway with a straight stair beside it and an enlarged west window. The upper storeys have been destroyed but the latrine turret added against the west end still stands high. To the east was an office or living room, probably with a chapel on the missing upper storey. North of it is a section of late medieval curtain walling containing a postern doorway looking out onto the base of the incomplete east range.

OTHER CASTLE SITES IN GOWER

BARLAND SS 582900 Ringwork 22m across. Ditch 2.5m deep. Excavated 1898.
CIL IFOR SS 507922 Damaged ringwork 40m by 30m at SE end of hillfort.
PENLLE'R SS 664094 This earthwork is described in Glamorgan section, p92.

GLOSSARY OF TERMS

ASHLAR - Masonry of blocks with even faces and square edges. BAILEY - Defensible court enclosed by a wall or palisade and ditch. BARBICAN - Defensible court, passage or porch in front of an entrance. BASTION - Flanking projection of the same height as the main wall. BUTTERY - A room where drink was stored. CORBEL - A projecting bracket supporting other stonework or a timber beam. CRENEL - A cut-away part of a parapet. A parapet so equipped on a secular building implied some degree of fortification. CURTAIN WALL - A high enclosing wall around a bailey. DRUM TOWER - A circular tower. EMBATTLED - Having a parapet with indentations (crenellations). HOARDING - Wooden gallery at a wall-top providing machicolations. JAMB - A side of a doorway, window or other opening. KEEP - A citadel or ultimate strongpoint. The term is not medieval and they were then called donjons or great towers (magnum turris in Latin). LIGHT - A compartment of a window. LOOP - A small, narrow opening for light or for the discharge of missiles. MACHICOLATION -A slot for dropping stones or firing missiles at assailants. MERLONS - The upstanding portions of a crenellated parapet. MOAT - A ditch, wet or dry, around an enclosure. MOTTE - A steep-sided, flat-topped mound, partly or wholly man-made. MULLION -A vertical member dividing the lights of a window. OILLET - A roundel at an extremity of a loop. ORIEL - A projecting bay containing windows. PARAPET - A wall for protection at any sudden drop. PISCINA - A stone basin for draining out a chalice after mass. PILASTER - A shallow buttress like a rectangular attached column. PLINTH - The projecting base of a wall, either battered (sloped) or stepped. PORTCULLIS - A wooden gate made to rise and fall in vertical grooves. POSTERN -A back entrance or lesser gateway. RERE-ARCH - Arch over the inner face of a window embrasure or doorway. RINGWORK - An embanked enclosure of more modest size than a bailey, generally bigger but less elevated than a motte summit. ROLL MOULDING - Moulding of circular or D-shaped section. SHELL KEEP - Small stone-walled enclosure on top of a motte. SOLAR - A lord's living room, sometimes also serving as his bedroom. TRANSOM - Horizontal member dividing top and bottom window lights. WALL-WALK A walkway on a wall top, protected by a parapet. WARD - A stone walled defensive enclosure.

PUBLIC ACCESS TO THE SIDES   Codes used in the gazetteers.

C Buildings in the care of Cadw to which an admission fee is payable.
F Ruins or earthworks to which there is free access at least during daylight hours.
O Buildings opened to the public by private owners, local councils, trusts, etc.
V Sites closely visible from roads, paths, churchyards, public open spaces, etc.

FURTHER READING

The Castles of Gower, Gower Society, 1970.
Norman Castles in Britain, Derek Renn, 1968.
Medieval Military Architecture, G.T.Clark, 1884.
Castles of the Welsh Princes, Paul R.Davis, 1988.
A History of the County of Glamorgan (several volumes).
A History of Monmouthshire (several volumes) Joseph Bradney.
Buildings of Wales: Glamorgan (1995) & Gwent (2000) vols, both by John Newman.
RCAHMW Inventories of Ancient Monuments in Glamorgan, Vols III & IV, 1981-2000
Periodicals: Morgannwg, Gwent Local History, Archeologia Cambrensis.
Guides or histories of the following castles are or were available: Abergavenny, Chepstow, Grosmont, Monmouth, Newport, Penhow, Raglan, Skenfrith, White, Beaupre, Caerphilly, Cardiff, Castell Coch, Coity, Ewenny, Fonmon, Llandaff, Newcastle Bridgend, St Donat's, St Fagans, Oystermouth, Weobley.